PLANTS

WEEDS
OF THE GLOBAL
GARDEN

John M. Randall &

Janet Marinelli

Editors

Invasive bull thistle, *Cirsium vulgare,* in
Yosemite Valley, with Half Dome in the
background.

FOR THE
ADVANCE
MENT OF
BOTANY
AND THE
SERVICE OF
THE CITY

BROOKLYN
BOTANIC
GARDEN
PUBLICATIONS
· MCMXCVI ·

Janet Marinelli
SERIES EDITOR

Beth Hanson
ASSOCIATE EDITOR

Bekka Lindstrom
ART DIRECTOR

Stephen K-M. Tim
VICE PRESIDENT, SCIENCE, LIBRARY & PUBLICATIONS

Judith D. Zuk
PRESIDENT

Elizabeth Scholtz
DIRECTOR EMERITUS

Handbook #149

Copyright © Winter 1996 by the Brooklyn Botanic Garden, Inc.

Handbooks in the 21st-Century Gardening Series, formerly Plants & Gardens,
are published quarterly at 1000 Washington Ave., Brooklyn, NY 11225.

Subscription included in Brooklyn Botanic Garden subscribing membership dues ($35.00 per year).

ISSN # 0362-5850 ISBN # 0-945352-95-6

Printed by Science Press, a division of the Mack Printing Group

COVER PHOTO: PURPLE LOOSESTRIFE OVERRUNS A STAND OF NATIVE CATTAIL IN A WETLAND

Table of Contents

Introduction

REDEFINING THE WEED

BY JANET MARINELLI

USED TO BE, gardens were tiny enclaves in a vast wilderness. Beleaguered gardeners struggled daily against the forces of nature, not the least of which were weeds—hence the traditional definition of a weed as any plant from outside the garden that ends up inside the garden where it isn't wanted. But, boy, have the tables turned. Today, around the globe, shrunken fragments of once-awesome wilderness are hemmed in by human-dominated land. Now it is *our* activities, including our gardens, that threaten natural areas and the creatures they harbor. Hundreds of species that we've carried from their native ranges to new areas, including prized horticultural plants, have overrun native vegetation. These have become the true weeds of the modern world.

People have been rearranging the planet's flora for centuries. Many of the exotic plants we've introduced by intention or accident have been beneficial to us and ecologically benign. But a small percentage have run rampant. Gaining a foothold first in areas disturbed by human activities, they moved into natural areas where they've not only driven out indigenous species but in the worst cases radically altered the ecosystems they've invaded.

In 1993, after an extensive review of exotic species, the Congressional Office of Technology Assessment (OTA) concluded that pest plants and animals have an effect not only on natural areas but also on agriculture, industry and human health. In its report, *Harmful Non-Indigenous Species in the United States*, the

Purple loosestrife in a garden and overrunning a wetland, blocked off into study plots by researchers. Thousands of non-indigenous plant species are known to persist outside of cultivation in the U.S. About 300 are truly invasive, and about half of these were brought here to beautify our gardens.

agency noted that from 1906 to 1991, just 79 problem plants and animals caused documented losses of $97 billion, and that a worst-case scenario for a mere 15 potentially high-impact species could cause another $134 billion in future economic losses.

Thousands of non-indigenous plant species are known to persist outside of cultivation in the United States. How many of these are plant invaders? In the course of researching this book, we tallied the species on the two most comprehensive national natural areas weed lists ever compiled: one of plants being reported as problems on Nature Conservancy preserves nationwide, and another compiled by the National Assocation of Exotic Pest Plant Councils, an umbrella organization of state groups concerned about the ecological impact of invasive non-native species. After submitting the combined list to various state weed authorities for their additions and subtractions, we arrived at a total of just over 300 plants invading wildlands in the 49 continental states and Canadian provinces. (We didn't have room for the plant invaders of Hawaii, which could easily fill an entire volume.) According to our calculations, about half of the 300 continental plant invaders were brought here to beautify our gardens. A much tinier fraction of native plants are showing signs of invasiveness, but there is considerable disagreement over why and what kind of threat they pose; this, too, is a subject for another volume.

The problem is surprisingly widespread. Hawaii, California and Florida appear to be the hardest hit, but few—if any—regions of the U.S. and southern Canada are without non-native pests. According to *The Flora of North America*, the most comprehensive reference on this continent's plants, one-fifth to one-third of all species growing north of Mexico have come from other continents.

This ground-breaking handbook focuses on 80 of the invasive plants used horticulturally. These include the most serious invasives, such as purple loose-strife, which are so widespread that they'd be found on any "most wanted list" of plant invaders. Others, such as baby's breath, are problems in a geographically limited area—in this case, Great Lakes dune systems—but threaten unique habitats or rare plants. A few, like dame's rocket, right now appear to be only slightly invasive but are on weed experts' "to watch" lists because it often takes decades for a plant to begin spreading out of control—and once invasives are well established they are extremely difficult to manage.

In the chapter that follows, co-editor John Randall, who regularly criss-crosses the country to study invasives for The Nature Conservancy, explains how problem plants damage natural areas and why some introduced species become pests while others don't. Next is a section on the tools and techniques to control invasive plants, from hand-pulling to prescribed burning to, as a last resort, chemical herbicides.

The core of the book is an encyclopedia of invasive species used horticulturally, which was written by many of North America's leading weed experts and natural areas managers from 20 states and the District of Columbia. The encyclopedia is organized by plant type: trees, shrubs, annuals and perennials, grasses, vines and aquatic plants. To find out which ones are problems in your area, look in the index and in individual encyclopedia entries under the section "Where has it spread?" Each plant write-up will not only help you identify invasives and understand their ecological impacts but also tell you which to avoid planting and how to control plants already on your property that threaten nearby natural areas.

Scientists don't yet know whether some invasives represent permanent threats to the Earth's biodiversity, or whether they will become less dominant over the long haul as the plant communities they've invaded change and mature. In any event, the most prudent course of action is to avoid planting these species—because when it comes to invasive plants, as land managers have learned the hard way, an ounce of prevention is worth a pound of cure.

Plant Invaders

HOW NON-NATIVE SPECIES INVADE & DEGRADE NATURAL AREAS

BY JOHN M. RANDALL

CHANGE IN PLANT COMMUNITIES is natural. New species move in as the climate changes and as soils build up and become richer or erode and become less fertile. The arrival of new species may be the result of a single catastrophic event like a hurricane, or of gradual change over thousands of years. Humans have vastly accelerated the movement of plants, carrying thousands of species that could not have crossed natural barriers like oceans, mountain ranges and deserts to new areas. Species that have flourished and spread on their own only after people transported them across barriers they could not otherwise surmount are considered non-natives. In many areas these plants have overwhelmed the native plants and animals. Non-native species are responsible for most damaging invasions, but a far smaller number of natives also have invaded and degraded new habitats.

HOW PLANTS GET AROUND

Unlike animals, plants are sessile, meaning individuals can't move from place to place. However, many plants have mechanisms that enable their seeds, spores or other propagules to move and colonize new areas far from the parent plant. Some seeds are shot explosively from their pods, some are carried by wind or water. Others are caught and carried on the fur or feathers of passing animals. Animals eat the nourishing fruits of some plants and may deposit the seeds, unharmed, at distant sites.

The distances seeds travel can be astonishing. Most native Hawaiian plants evolved from colonists that crossed thousands of miles of ocean from the Americas or Asia. Following the retreat of the glaciers roughly 10,000 years ago, many species moved northward, colonizing the newly available ground. Among them were several oak species which migrated, probably with the help of hungry blue jays, from the southeastern U.S. to southern Canada, an average of 380 yards each year.

But no animal surpasses humans in dispersing plants, and we've been doing it for a long time. The "Iceman," whose 5,200-year-old corpse was recently discovered on a glacier on the Italian-Austrian border, had stuffed grasses into his shoes to keep his feet warm and was carrying a sloe berry. Human transport of plants and animals—and disease organisms—increased exponentially as our transportation technology developed. People transported and introduced some non-native species intentionally, for food, fiber, medicine, ornament or scientific curiosity. European species were advertised for sale in the U.S. as early as the Colonial period, and by the late 1800s seed catalogs listed hundreds of non-native ornamentals. Seeds of other plants were introduced accidentally in sacks of seed grain, wool or cotton, in mud stuck to machinery or in ship ballast. Human activities like farming, irrigation, forestry and mining have made it easier for these non-native species to become established by removing native vegetation, disturbing the soil and altering the availability of water and nutrients.

Intentional and unintentional introductions continue at a rapid pace today, accelerated by the recent rise in international trade. For example, before humans arrived in Hawaii, new plant species are believed to have become established at the rate of one every 10,000 years. For the past 200 years, we have been bringing new species to the islands at a rate *one million times higher.*

Melaleuca, introduced as an ornamental tree at the turn of the century, invades herbaceous wetlands in South Florida, forming solid stands that crowd out other species, and converting marsh into swamp forest where native species can't survive.

THE DAMAGE THEY DO

In their new environments, a relatively small number of non-native species have reproduced and spread without further human assistance, and only a fraction of these have become invasive pests in their new habitats. Yet the economic damage to agriculture and the environment caused by a few hundred or so of these plant invaders is staggering.

Invasives reproduce rapidly and can form stands that exclude nearly all other plants. In the process they damage natural areas, altering ecosystem processes, displacing native species, hybridizing with natives and changing their genetic makeup, and supporting other non-native plants, animals and pathogens.

Plants that change fundamental ecosystem processes such as the frequency of wildfires, the availability of water or nutrients and the rate of soil erosion cause the

9

severest problems. They "change the rules of the game" and many native plants and animals can't compete. Melaleuca (*Melaleuca quinquenervia*), introduced for forestry and as an ornamental, has invaded herbaceous wetlands in south Florida, forming solid stands and crowding out nearly all other species, moderating soil temperatures under their deep shade and drawing down the water table. The species has converted at least 450,000 acres of marsh into swamp forest, where native herbaceous plants can't survive. In the Southwest, tamarisks (*Tamarix* species) invade wetland and streamside areas and also likely lower water tables, shrinking or eliminating the surface water habitats of native plants and animals. Dense stands of tamarisk trap more sediments than those of native vegetation, altering the shape, carrying capacity and flooding cycle of watercourses.

Invaders that don't change basic ecosystem processes cause other problems. In forested areas, trees such as Norway maple (*Acer platanoides*) grow into the canopy, as do vines like Japanese honeysuckle (*Lonicera japonica*), where they shade out or topple trees; shrubs like the bush honeysuckles (*Lonicera* species) and buckthorns (*Rhamnus cathartica* and *R. frangula*) take over the mid-story, while herbaceous species such as garlic mustard (*Alliaria petiolata*) colonize and dominate the groundlayer. Prairies and other grasslands across the continent are severely infested by non-native species, many of them serious crop and rangeland pests like leafy spurge (*Euphorbia esula*) and yellow starthistle (*Centaurea solstitialis*). In wetlands in the northern third of the U.S. and southern Canada, purple loosestrife (*Lythrum salicaria*) forms large, dense stands, eliminating the open water areas that waterfowl require and elsewhere displacing native plants that feed and shelter wildlife.

Some invaders hybridize with natives and with time could eliminate native genetic strains. Non-native white mulberry (*Morus alba*), now widespread in eastern North America, hybridizes with the native red mulberry (*Morus rubra*).

Some invasives reduce or eliminate the very species and communities that national parks and nature preserves were set aside to protect. Rare species appear to be particularly vulnerable to the changes wrought by non-natives. For example, 30 of California's 53 federally listed endangered plant species are threatened by non-native invaders.

Invasive plants can also promote invasions by non-native animals. Leaf litter from the Chinese tallow tree (*Sapium sebiferum*), a pest in bottomland forests and swamps along the U.S. Gulf and lower Atlantic coasts, alters rates of nutrient cycling, boosting populations of the non-native isopod *Armadillium vulgare* while depressing populations of native soil invertebrates.

THE MOST VULNERABLE AREAS

One question that has long intrigued scientists is why some areas appear to be more prone to invasion than others. Many hypotheses have been advanced but there are few solid answers. Nearly half of the plant species growing wild in Hawaii, which like many remote islands in temperate and tropical areas is vulnerable to invasion, are non-native; New York, with 36 percent, has the highest percentage of non-native species among the mainland states. One explanation for the vulnerability of remote islands is that they had no large native herbivores, and so native plants did not evolve spines or foul-tasting chemicals that would have made them unpalatable to the pigs, cattle, sheep and other grazers brought by humans. Islands and peninsulas such as southern Florida may also be vulnerable because they have relatively low numbers of native species or are missing certain distinctive plant groups. Some, but not all, researchers believe that this leaves "empty niches" that new arrivals can exploit. For example in Hawaii, where no mangroves are native, a species introduced from Florida in 1902 has become a nasty pest.

WHAT MAKES A PLANT INVASIVE?

Researchers are also working to discover why some non-natives become invasive while others don't. According to one theory, some probably succeed because they aren't held in check by the predators and parasites that controlled their numbers in their original lands. And because they're not under attack, they may be able to redirect energy they would have invested in producing the toxic chemicals or spines to growth and reproduction. Native plants, by contrast, cannot lower their defenses or they will be attacked by the pests that evolved along with them. Two major studies found the best predictor was whether a plant was known to be invasive in another part of the world.

Recent work has found that species that share some or all of the following characteristics are most likely to be invasive:

• They produce many small seeds and begin reproducing within their first few years.

• Their seeds are dispersed by animals.

• They can reproduce both by seed and vegetative growth.

• They have long flowering and fruiting periods.

• They have no special seed germination requirements, such as a period of exposure to cold.

Carefully controlled fires can sometimes be used to contain the spread of invasive plants. This method is most effective on large plots of land such as parks and preserves, and should only be undertaken by people who have had proper training.

Some evidence also indicates the following characteristics may be predictors of a species's invasiveness:

- Self-fertility or self-compatibility, meaning a species can fertilize itself. (Many self-incompatible species are also successful invaders, however.)
- Large native north-south ranges in Europe and Asia. Species with large native ranges appear to be well adapted to a variety of climate and soil conditions and therefore more likely to find suitable habitat in a new area.
- No close relatives (for example, in the same genus) among any native species.
- Has been introduced on a large scale or repeatedly into a new range.

Preliminary data from one interesting study shows that invasive species are likely to have relatively small amounts of DNA in their cell nuclei. Apparently, the cells in these plants are able to divide and multiply more quickly and consequently the entire plant can grow more rapidly than species with higher cellular DNA content. This gives them a leg up in disturbed sites.

Many decades often pass between the first introduction of a plant and its eventual rapid spread. As far as we know, Atlantic cord grass (*Spartina alterniflora*) was present in small patches in a few spots on the Pacific Coast for 50 years or more before it began to spread aggressively. In other words, species that rarely spread today may turn out to be troublesome 40 or more years from now. And that's why it's so important that we find some way to determine which species are most likely to become invasive. Then we will be able to act while their populations are still small—and controllable.

Tools & Techniques

CHEMICAL-FREE CONTROLS

BY BETH HANSON

NATURE HAS INGENIOUSLY designed plants and animals to spread their genes as far and wide as possible—and some are better at this than others. For gardeners this means constantly having to decide which plants we can live with and which ones have to go. Techniques to rid the garden of the unwanted range from benign "mechanical" methods to the riskier chemical controls. If a non-chemical method will work for you, use it. You don't want to unnecessarily expose desirable plants to herbicides that may be just as poisonous to them as to the weeds. Unless an infestation of invasives is so severe, or your property so extensive that mechanical controls are impractical (as on many public and park lands), you may well be able to banish the weeds using one of the following non-chemical techniques.

HAND-PULLING

Pulling weeds by hand, probably the most ancient weed removal technique, works best with smaller annual and biennial plants before they have had a chance to produce and spread their seed, especially when the soil is damp. If possible, pull up the entire root system of the plant, but try not to disturb the surrounding soil as this will invite further invasion. If you do disturb the soil, replace the litter on top of it, leaving the area looking as much as possible as it did when you arrived. Take care not to trample native plants or to compact the soil; this may be easier if you sit on an inner tube while weeding to distribute your weight more evenly.

WEEDING TOOLS

Two small companies in the West now produce tools designed specifically for pulling shrubs such as Scotch broom, tamarisk, thistle, honeysuckle, holly and Russian olive. The Weed Wrench and the Root Jack are both basically lever arms with a pincher or clamp at the bottom to grip the stem of the plant. Once the stem is caught in the grip, the user leans back, tightening the clamp in the process, and after a little rocking, the entire plant comes up, roots included. If the soil is wet, put a board under the corner of the arm so it does not sink into the ground. (The Weed Wrench is available from New Tribe, 541-476-9492, the Root Jack from Mike Giacomini, 415-454-0849.)

CANE KNIFE

Sugar-cane cutters use these knives to cut through thick cane stems. They're similar to machetes but have a deeper blade (use them with care!) and a hook on the back to pick up what's just been cut. Cane knives work well on large herbaceous plants such as nettle, lantana, mullein, blackberry and bolted second-year thistle, as well as young trees and shrubs. With practice, you'll be able to cut through a 1- to 2-inch thick stem. Cane knives can be hard to obtain in the cooler regions of the continent. If you have trouble finding one, a machete will work almost as well.

THREE-PRONGED CLAW

This common tool is useful for pulling out vines such as vinca, English ivy and other plants that have lots of shallow roots. Cut into the patch of vines with clippers, then drag out the vine with this claw. When you're done, rake the soil back into place. Clearing an area with a claw can require a lot of work, but less so than hand-pulling in many cases.

GIRDLING

By cutting and pulling a 2-inch wide strip of bark away from the circumference of a tree trunk, you stop the flow of sugars through its cambium, and the tree will eventually die. The cut should be deep enough that you've cut through the thin oniony layer under the bark around the trunk, the cambium. Girdling works on many types of trees such as pines, some species of oak and maples. Most shrubs have so many stems that this method is impractical. A good knife with a blunt blade is the best tool for this job. Some gardening supply catalogs sell girdling knives.

MULCHING

Many seeds need light to germinate and become established. If you cover the ground with a layer of non-living material (hay, straw, grass clippings, wood chips, plastic film), you will deprive the seeds of light, and thereby prevent unwanted seedlings from surviving.

MOWING

Some weeds can be controlled by mowing. Annuals are especially susceptible if mown shortly before they set flower, since by that time they have already used most of their root reserves to produce the buds. Mowing works best in meadows and grasslands. In woody areas you achieve the same effect using a weed whip (you can also mow more precisely), but be careful not to inadvertently girdle nearby trees. In backyards, it's almost always possible to kill weeds without herbicides if you are persistent and willing to mow at short enough intervals to exhaust the energy in the weeds' roots.

HEAT

Hot water: In urban and home situations, try pouring boiling water on the weeds that sprout between cracks in walks and drives. Deeply rooted plants are likely to come back unless the hot water reaches the roots. At schools and other public places where herbicides are out of the question, steam injectors are used to kill weeds.

Propane: This method basically roasts seedlings but you need to get them when they are most susceptible—before they develop extensive roots.

Prescribed burning: This method is most appropriate for large plots of land such as prairies and meadows, to kill those plants that won't come back after their foliage has been destroyed by fire (juniper or red cedar, *Juniperis virginiana*, for example, is a common invader of grasslands). Prescribed burns should only be conducted by a properly trained and certified burn crew. Contact your local extension agent if you think this control is appropriate for your situation.

TILLING

For those with large areas hopelessly infested with invasives, plowing the soil can be effective. By using the right type of plow to turn the soil in your area, you can cut the plants' roots and tip them upside down beneath a cover of soil, in effect smothering them. Tilling is comparable to digging out invasives—and whatever natives remain in the area as well—on a huge scale.

To Spray or Not to Spray

THAT IS THE QUESTION!

BY HENRY W. ART

*"Whether 'tis nobler in the mind to suffer
The slings and arrows of outrageous fortune,
Or to take arms against a sea of troubles,
And by opposing end them?"*

YOU DON'T HAVE TO be a Shakespeare scholar to know that the Prince of Denmark is not contemplating a castle grounds filled with invasive exotics when he utters these lines. However, Hamlet's quandary of whether to suffer or to take up arms is felt by many of us confronted by decisions about a sea of troubling, persistent, aggressive weeds that have the potential to reduce the diversity of landscapes once dominated by native species.

As an ecologist I am particularly sensitive about recommending the use of herbicides to control unwanted plants because there is a tendency to overuse these poisons to create sterile landscapes without much regard to the environmental consequences. I certainly do not advocate the use of herbicides of any sort on the plant community we have come to call the lawn. Frankly, I find a diverse lawn with a mixture of grasses, clovers, ground-ivy and other green, living plants (regardless of their origins) to be both aesthetically pleasing and easily maintained by periodic mowing. The added benefit is that when a dry spell eventually occurs, there is always something green that survives.

Mechanical removal or non-chemical treatments should be the first line of defense against invasive exotics. Sometimes these are as simple as hand weeding, repeated mowings before the plants set seed or smothering the weeds with layers of newspapers or black plastic sheeting for several months. Propane weeders, which kill plants by searing them with a flame, should be used with extreme caution. Once I set the lowest whorl of branches of a white pine on fire when I inadvertently ignited the soil humus layer in addition to the shrubs I was attempting to kill. My wife graciously offered to call the volunteer fire department, but I was spared the embarrassment (and the loss of valuable trees) when I extinguished the smoky blaze with the aid of a garden hose—I was lucky.

These measures may not work with all invasive species. Some aggressive weeds, such as Japanese knotweed (*Fallopia japonica*), common reed (*Phragmites australis*, sometimes called *P. communis*) and Japanese honeysuckle (*Lonicera japonica*) have very deep or extensive rhizomes that are nearly impossible to dig out unless you use a back hoe or steam shovel. Furthermore, there are real problems with disposing of the soil, which is laden with buried seeds and fragments of live plants that could become reestablished. Under these circumstances the judicious use of the least persistent, most effective and environment-friendly (if that is not an oxymoron) herbicide may be warranted.

I have used glyphosate herbicide (marketed under such names as Roundup, Kleen-up and Rodeo) to eradicate poison ivy (*Rhus radicans*) along the roadside on my property, having grown over the years terribly allergic to the plant. This non-selective herbicide is taken up through the leaves and translocated to the roots, where it disrupts the plant's metabolism. It generally takes several days before wilting of the plant is visible, and several weeks for the plant to die. The great advantage of glyphosate is that it is rapidly broken down by microorganisms in the soil, so it does not persist in the environment. Another group of relatively environment-friendly herbicides is formulated from soap-based fatty acids (marketed under such names as SharpShooter and Scythe) that kill foliage by entering leaves and disrupting plant membranes. Within several hours the shoots of the plant wither and dry out. Soap-based fatty acids are rapidly dissipated in the soil and affect only plants that are contacted.

One windless Sunday morning in August I sneaked out at 7:00 a.m. to apply herbicide using a low-pressure spray tank. Being careful to administer the poi-

Mechanical removal should be the first line of defense against invasive exotics. However, such measures may not work with all invasive species. In these cases the judicious use of the least persistent, most effective and environment-friendly herbicide may be warranted.

son only to the leaves of the target plants, I carefully worked my way along the edge of my meadow. As luck would have it, the chairman of the local conservation commission drove by on her way home from an early morning bird walk and stopped to check up on what this ecologist was doing with a spray tank. I was discovered! After my blushing subsided we did have an opportunity to discuss the rational use of herbicides.

A few important things to keep in mind before you apply these poisons:

• Read all of the instructions that come with the packaging *before* purchasing an herbicide to make sure you buy one that will be effective on the species you want to kill.

• Use only herbicides that are recommended to kill the species that you wish to control, and mix them according to directions. Stronger herbicide is *not* better.

• Dress appropriately with protective clothing to avoid skin contact with herbicides. Long-sleeved shirts, trousers, rubber gloves and boots are recommended.

• Apply only during the season that the herbicide is effective. Many plants are most susceptible to herbicides during that period of their growth when substances are being translocated out of the leaves and into the roots—usually toward the end of the summer. Some woody plants are best attacked by cutting

continues on page 22

HERBICIDES

USE THEM WITH CARE

ACTIVE INGREDIENT	BRAND NAMES
Clopyralid	Stinger, Reclaim, Transline, Curtail
Glyphosate	Roundup, Rodeo (for aquatic areas)
Imazapyr	Arsenal
MCPA	Rhomene, Rhonox
Picloram	Tordon, Grazon
Triclopyr	Garlon 3A, Garlon 4, Turflon
2,4-D	Weedar, Weedone, Weed-b-Gon

Some of these brands contain lower concentrations of the active ingredient and are available for use in residential areas. You can generally find them in garden centers and hardware stores.

Most home gardens are small enough that gardeners can control invasive plants without using herbicides. If your property is large or you have a more intractable weed problem, use herbicides only as a last resort and after studying the label to be sure you are buying the appropriate chemical. Before resorting to the more toxic chemical herbicides, try relatively environment-friendly formulations made from soap-based fatty acids. Use any herbicide in the proper manner, described on its label, to protect nearby plants, animals and waterways from harm. The chemicals below are among the controls cited in the Encyclopedia of Invasive Plants beginning on page 23.

EFFECTIVE AGAINST	CAUTION!
Members of the sunflower, buckwheat and pea families	Can leach into soils and persist in environment
Roundup: Annual and perennial grasses and broadleaf weeds; Rodeo: above-surface weeds in aquatic areas	Non-selective, can kill beneficial species; the surfactant in Roundup is toxic to fish and other aquatic organisms
Kills a wide variety of annual and perennial weeds, trees, vines and brambles	Spray drift or "leakage" from roots of treated plants can damage those nearby; persistent in soils, will kill seedlings
Broadleaf weeds	Drift can damage other nearby desirable broadleaf plants; cotton, grapes and tomatoes are particularly sensitive
Kills broadleaf weeds, woody plants	Relatively water soluble and very persistent in the environment, "a method of last resort"
Woody brush, annual and perennial broadleaf weeds and root-sprouting species such as ash and tamarisk	Leachable in soils; Garlon 3A and other amine formulations are highly alkaline and can severely damage eye tissue
Kills broadleaf weeds, woody plants	Can damage other nearby desirable broadleaf plants; cotton, grapes and tomatoes are particularly sensitive

HOW TO APPLY HERBICIDES

BASAL BARK TREATMENT: Herbicide is applied to young, smooth-barked trees in a 6- to 12-inch band around the entire trunk about a foot above ground. Not effective on older trees or those with thick bark.

CUT-STUMP APPLICATION: Herbicide is applied to the cut stumps of trees or shrubs and need only make contact with the living inner bark layer, not the woody interior tissue.

FOLIAR SPRAYING: Herbicide, which may include a surfactant to help it adhere to leaves and penetrate the leaf tissue, is sprayed onto the foliage of the target plant. Avoid overspraying onto other plants or allowing herbicide to drift.

WICK APPLICATION: Herbicide is wiped onto foliage and stems with a sponge or wick on a long handle, allowing targeted application with less drift and drip than foliar sprays.

FRILL: Herbicide is applied to cut areas in trunk made by girdling (see page 15) or hacking with a machete.

the shoot, painting herbicide on the cut stump and covering the stump with black plastic sheeting.

• Do not apply herbicides in hot weather—avoid spraying at midday or in the afternoon in summer as some herbicides are easily volatilized and may move off the target plant as a cloud of vapor only to condense elsewhere. Be careful to treat only leaves of plants you desire to kill. A low-pressure tank with a controlled spray, or applying the herbicide with a ½-inch paint brush work well. If you have a large area to treat, you can apply it to the plant surfaces using your hand, protected by a heavy rubber glove over which you put a cotton glove or an old sock. Then mix the herbicide in a small plastic bucket, dip in your protected hand, squeeze out the excess and apply to the target leaves, being careful not to spill or splash.

• Be prepared to repeat treatments. Species like mile-a-minute (*Polygonum perfoliatum*) are rarely controlled by a single application.

Finally, when considering whether to spray, or not to spray, you can do no better than to keep the following guidelines of the Connecticut Department of Transportation Herbicide Program in mind: Apply the least amount of the safest chemical to specific species of plants in a specific area at the appropriate time to obtain a desired 90 percent control.

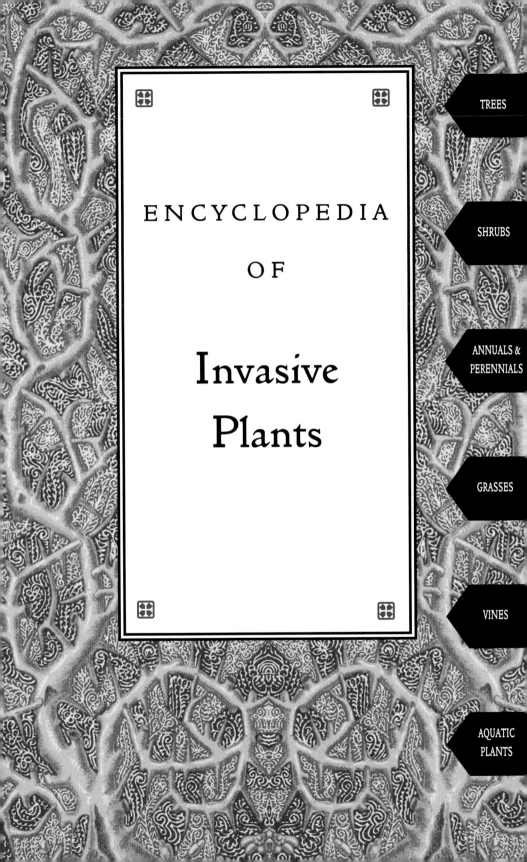

ENCYCLOPEDIA

OF

Invasive
Plants

TREES

SHRUBS

ANNUALS &
PERENNIALS

GRASSES

VINES

AQUATIC
PLANTS

TREES

Earleaf acacia has become an envi-ronmental pest in the southern half of Florida, where it invades what lit-tle undisturbed pine rockland habi-tat remains. Because it is fast grow-ing, it can readily shade out sun-lov-ing native pineland species.

WHAT DOES IT LOOK LIKE?
Earleaf acacia grows to about 40 feet tall and is easily recognized by its sickle-shaped petioles (leaf stalks), which resemble simple leaves. Very small yel-low flowers are produced in spring, sum-mer and fall and are followed by contort-ed green fruits that turn brown with age.

WHERE DID IT COME FROM? WHERE HAS IT SPREAD?
Earleaf acacia is a native of tropical northern Australia and New Guinea. It is cultivated in dry tropical and warm temperate regions and is a common landscape tree in southern Florida. It readily escapes cultivation in southern Florida and is principally found in dis-turbed sites, such as roadsides and vacant lots, as well as in undisturbed pine rockland habitat.

WHAT PROBLEMS DOES IT CAUSE?
Earleaf acacia has become an environ-mental pest in the southern half of Florida. Its ability to invade what little undisturbed pine rockland habitat remains is cause for concern because it is fast growing and can shade out sun-loving native pineland species. Earleaf acacia produces brittle wood and is highly susceptible to wind damage, making large specimens hazardous to people and property during Florida's tropical storms and hurricanes.

HOW CAN IT BE CONTROLLED?
Earleaf acacia should be basally treat-ed with a triclopyr herbicide mixed with an oil diluent. Like all exotic trees, it should not be hand-pulled in pine rockland habitat as this can cause soil disturbance and invite further inva-sion by exotic plants. Prescribed fire in pineland areas will help control seedlings and saplings of this species.

Roger L. Hammer, Metropolitan Dade County Park and Recreation Department

What does it look like?

This small tree may reach a height of 20 feet, with a few large branches near the base and a broad crown. Like most maples it has simple leaves growing opposite each other on the branch. Amur maple's leaves have shallow lobes and double-toothed edges. Pale yellow, fragrant flowers appear in loose clusters with young leaves in the spring. Reddish, two-winged, inch-long fruits mature in late summer.

Where did it come from? Where has it spread?

Amur maple is a native of central and northern China, Manchuria and Japan, and was introduced into the U.S. and Canada in the 1860s. It is best adapted to northern areas with relatively cool summers, where it requires little maintenance and does well in shade. It is occasionally planted, but only a few cultivars are available. Though reported as rarely spreading from cultivation, extensive wild populations have been found in Illinois and Missouri.

What problems does it cause?

Amur maple has the potential to become a major weed in northeastern U.S. and adjacent Canada. One small tree can produce more than 5,000 two-seeded fruits, which are widely disseminated by the wind. In successional fields and open woods, it displaces native shrubs and understory trees. In prairie habitats it can shade out native species.

TREES

By some reports Amur maple rarely spreads from cultivation, yet extensive wild populations can be found in Illinois and Missouri. It has the potential to become a major weed in the northeastern U.S. and Canada.

How can it be controlled?

Amur maples produce large quantities of seed, so they should not be planted near natural areas. Wild populations are easily controlled by cutting and treating the stumps with a glyphosate herbicide. Shoots sometimes resprout from stumps but not roots. Amur maple is also susceptible to fire, commonly used to control woody invasions in prairies.

John E. Ebinger, Botany Department, Eastern Illinois University

TREES

Norway maple, the most planted street tree in the U.S., is outcompeting native sugar maples and beeches along the East Coast and in Ontario and the Northwest.

WHAT DOES IT LOOK LIKE?

Norway maple closely resembles its native relative, the sugar maple (*Acer saccharum*), with the hand-shaped leaf represented on the Canadian flag. Norway maple can be distinguished from sugar maple by its milky sap (break a leaf to check), smooth leaf underside, upright green flower clusters and regularly grooved bark. The fall foliage is yellow, never red, while that of sugar maple varies from yellow to orange to red. However, the foliage of the popular "crimson" varieties of Norway maple is maroon-red all summer long.

WHERE DID IT COME FROM? WHERE HAS IT SPREAD?

A native of Eurasia from southern Scandinavia to northern Iran, Norway maple was introduced as an ornamental shade tree in Philadelphia in 1762. Today, it is the most planted street tree in the U.S. It spreads by seed into both open lots and forest preserves. Invasions are reported from Massachusetts to Washington, D.C., in Ontario and also in the Pacific Northwest. However, Norway maple is probably more widespread than we realize, because it often is mistaken for its native cousin, the sugar maple.

WHAT PROBLEMS DOES IT CAUSE?

Norway maple can transform the native woodland communities it invades by outcompeting native sugar maples and beeches, thanks to its tolerance of shade and efficient use of water and nutrients. In addition, there is less wildflower diversity under the dense Norway maple canopy than under native trees.

HOW CAN IT BE CONTROLLED?

Urge planning boards to ban Norway maple. Seedlings and saplings can be hand-pulled or dug out; they quickly resprout unless roots are pulled up along with the stem. Mature trees should be cut down as close to the base as possible.

Sara L. Webb, Department of Biology, Drew University, New Jersey

Ailanthus has escaped cultivation from Massachusetts and southern Ontario to Texas and northern Florida, forming extensive thickets that displace native vegetation. It is also invasive along streamsides in the West.

TREES

WHAT DOES IT LOOK LIKE?

Ailanthus is a deciduous tree that grows up to 90 feet tall, with a broad, spreading crown of few branches. It has gray, relatively smooth bark, and 1- to 3-foot long leaves divided into 12 to 30 pointed leaflets. They resemble sumac leaflets but usually have one to four small round glands on their undersides. Depending on the area, ailanthus blooms between April and July with small, greenish flowers at the ends of the new shoots. The flowers develop into several separate fruits, each a papery wing with a single flattened seed in the center. These linger on the tree well into winter.

WHERE DID IT COME FROM? WHERE HAS IT SPREAD?

A native of eastern China, ailanthus was introduced as an ornamental tree by the 1780s. In the East, it is now found in the wild from Massachusetts and southern Ontario to Texas and northern Florida. In the West, it is widely but more discontinuously distributed and is most abundant from New Mexico west to California and north to Washington. It is primarily found in disturbed, semi-natural habitats, but can also occur in riparian (streamside) and other naturally disturbed habitats.

WHAT PROBLEMS DOES IT CAUSE?

Ailanthus produces abundant root sprouts that can develop into extensive thickets and displace native vegetation. In urban areas it is a maintenance problem for landscapers.

HOW CAN IT BE CONTROLLED?

When cut, ailanthus will produce vigorous stump and root sprouts. Repeated (and persistent) cutting of these can kill the tree. Much more effective control can be obtained by using basal bark application on small trees or cutting larger ones and immediately brushing the fresh-cut surface of the stem with a full-strength glyphosate herbicide.

John Hunter, Department of Biological Sciences, State University of New York, Brockport

TREES

Birds distribute bishopwood seeds into disturbed sites—roadsides and neglected lots—in southern Florida. The tree also invades the state's undisturbed hardwood forests, forming dense shade and crowding out native trees. Its invasive nature became clear following the destruction of native hardwood forests by Hurricane Andrew in 1992.

WHAT DOES IT LOOK LIKE?

Bishopwood is a large tree that grows to about 40 feet. Its dark green leaves are divided into three large, leathery leaflets with toothed margins. Female trees produce large quantities of hanging, grape-like clusters of brown fruit, each about the size of a pea.

WHERE DID IT COME FROM? WHERE HAS IT SPREAD?

Bishopwood is native to India, Malaysia, Polynesia and other parts of tropical Asia. It was introduced in the early 1900s as a fast-growing shade tree in southern Florida and other tropical and warm temperate regions. Birds distribute the seeds into hardwood forests and disturbed sites such as roadsides and neglected lots in southern Florida.

WHAT PROBLEMS DOES IT CAUSE?

This tree readily invades undisturbed hardwood forests in Florida, forming dense shade and crowding out native trees. Once the tree is firmly established, seedlings will appear throughout the understory. Bishopwood became a noticeable problem following the destruction of the native hardwood forests in southern Florida by Hurricane Andrew in 1992.

HOW CAN IT BE CONTROLLED?

Male trees in the landscape pose no problems, but female trees should be destroyed to ensure that fruits are not carried to natural areas by birds. Hand-pull young seedlings, and treat older trees basally with a triclopyr herbicide mixed with an oil diluent.

Roger L. Hammer, Metropolitan Dade County Park and Recreation Department

TREES

WHAT DOES IT LOOK LIKE?

Paper mulberry is a tree or tall shrub that can reach 50 feet in height. Its rounded, spreading canopy has made it a popular shade tree. The bark is gray. Broad, oval leaves are borne along slightly hairy twigs and are a dull, rough green above and woolly beneath. Leaves vary from unlobed to deeply lobed and are coarsely toothed, except at the base of the leaf or lobes. Male and female trees flower in June. Female flowers are red, and are followed by globular, brick-red fruits, while male flowers are borne in long, cylindrical structures called catkins.

WHERE DID IT COME FROM? WHERE HAS IT SPREAD?

A native of China and perhaps Japan, paper mulberry was brought to eastern North America as an ornamental. It escaped from cultivation and today is found from the Northeast west to Missouri and southward to Arkansas and neighboring states.

Paper mulberry has escaped cultivation from the Northeast west to Missouri, and southward.

WHAT PROBLEMS DOES IT CAUSE?

Paper mulberry colonizes disturbed areas; birds are the main means of transport for the highly viable seeds. After sprouting, the trees grow quickly, providing cover and food for birds. Paper mulberry is so successful because of its tolerance of stress, including drought and pollution.

HOW CAN IT BE CONTROLLED?

Anecdotal evidence suggests that pruning enhances the growth of this tree. Pulling or digging out small trees may prove effective. Larger trees can be cut off close to the ground and covered with black plastic to prevent resprouting. A basal bark treatment of triclopyr may also be effective.

Carolyn M. Thurman, The Nature Conservancy, Pennsylvania Chapter

TREES

Australian pine readily colonizes mangrove habitat, rocky shorelines and sandy beach dunes. It is a major environmental pest in Florida.

WHAT DOES IT LOOK LIKE?

Australian pine is a single-trunked tree that grows to 80 feet or more. It is a flowering plant in the beefwood family but produces green twigs resembling pine needles, which are jointed and separate easily to reveal the true leaves. These look like minuscule teeth surrounding the joint. Round, woody, spiny "cones" are produced twice yearly, each containing numerous winged seeds.

WHERE DID IT COME FROM? WHERE HAS IT SPREAD?

Australian pine is a native of Malaysia, southern Asia, Oceania and coastal Queensland, Australia. Introduced in the late 1800s, it is a major environmental pest in Florida.

WHAT PROBLEMS DOES IT CAUSE?

Australian pine is salt-tolerant and readily colonizes mangrove habitat, rocky shorelines and sandy beach dunes as well as sites far inland, especially disturbed sites. It can form dense single-species stands, crowding out native vegetation and eliminating the food sources of wildlife. On dunes, its shallow roots inhibit nest building by sea turtles and in southern Florida have even disrupted nesting American crocodiles. The tree releases large amounts of pollen, causing human respiratory problems.

HOW CAN IT BE CONTROLLED?

On dunes seedlings and young saplings can be hand-pulled. Mature trees are extremely susceptible to triclopyr herbicides mixed with an oil diluent, which should be sprayed in a band around the base of the trunk. Cut trees down while they're alive (dead wood is extremely difficult to cut) and spray the cut stump with a triclopyr herbicide–water mixture (50/50). Prescribed fire can eradicate this tree in pine forests and other fire-tolerant communities.

Roger L. Hammer, Metropolitan Dade County Park and Recreation Department

TREES

Salt-tolerant carrot wood easily invades damp places such as tropical hardwood hammocks throughout Florida, where it forms dense thickets.

WHAT DOES IT LOOK LIKE?

Carrot wood is easily recognized by its evenly pinnate (feather-like), compound leaves with six to ten leathery leaflets. It is a medium-sized, fast-growing tree that produces small, greenish white flowers in autumn and winter and three-lobed fruit in mid-summer.

WHERE DID IT COME FROM? WHERE HAS IT SPREAD?

Carrot wood is native to Australia and has become a popular landscape tree because it grows and produces shade quickly. It was introduced into Florida in 1968 as a nursery offering. It is spread by birds, and is salt-tolerant, easily invading cool, damp places such as tropical hardwood hammocks.

WHAT PROBLEMS DOES IT CAUSE?

Carrot wood can quickly invade both disturbed and undisturbed areas where it forms dense thickets that crowd out native vegetation. This tree, while relatively new to the landscape trade, is spreading rapidly and has the potential to become a major pest in tropical landscapes.

HOW CAN IT BE CONTROLLED?

The best control is to find the source tree and control it quickly. A basal bark application of a triclopyr herbicide mixed with a oil diluent works well. Seedlings can be hand-pulled.

Sandra Vardaman Wells, Metropolitan Dade County Park and Recreation Department

TREES

Bluegum, a prolific producer of fire-prone litter, is very invasive in many wildland settings, especially grasslands and shrublands of coastal California, where it displaces native vegetation and reduces biodiversity.

WHAT DOES IT LOOK LIKE?

Bluegum eucalyptus is often over 110 feet tall with a straight trunk, shedding bark and aromatic foliage. Young stems are squared and bear soft, oval leaves, while older leaves are waxy blue and sickle-shaped and hang vertically. Creamy white to yellow flowers appear from December to May. The 1-inch diameter fruits are woody, ribbed and blue-gray in color.

WHERE DID IT COME FROM? WHERE HAS IT SPREAD?

A native of Australia, bluegum was first cultivated as an ornamental in California. Since 1870 it has been widely planted as a windbreak and for lumber and pulpwood production. It does especially well in locations with Mediterranean climates, such as parts of California.

WHAT PROBLEMS DOES IT CAUSE?

Bluegum is very messy, producing large quantities of litter—bark, small limbs, twigs and leaves—which make it harder for understory plants to become established. The litter also creates a fire hazard that is especially dangerous in mixed wildland/urban areas. In both calm and stormy conditions, tree limbs often fall, creating a potential safety problem. Bluegum is very invasive in many wildland settings, especially grasslands and shrublands of coastal California, displacing native vegetation and reducing biodiversity.

HOW CAN IT BE CONTROLLED?

The stumps of cut trees contain vigorous buds that must be controlled. Control sprouting by stump grinding to a depth of 8 to 10 inches or by removing sprouts over a three-year period each time they reach 6 to 8 feet. Chemical control is often the best alternative for large numbers of trees. Immediate application of an herbicide such as glyphosate to the outer circumference of the stump surface is effective, especially if the tree is cut in fall.

David Boyd, California Department of Parks and Recreation, San Rafael

WHAT DO THEY LOOK LIKE?

Lofty fig, *F. altissima,* and banyan fig, *F. benghalensis,* are both large, spreading trees with aerial prop roots. Leaves of both species are large and broadly egg-shaped, but the veins on the underside of the leaf of lofty fig form a single vein while the veins on banyan fig leaves form a double V. In addition, the leaves of banyan fig are rounded at the tip and hairy on the lower sides, whereas lofty fig has hairless leaves with pointed tips. Fruit of both species are about ½ inch in diameter, but those of the lofty fig are yellow or orange while banyan fig produces red fruit. Both species can grow to 50 to 90 feet.

Laurel fig, *F. microcarpa,* is a large tree with a dense canopy of small, glossy, leathery leaves averaging 2 to 3 inches in length. The tree has a spreading growth habit with numerous aerial roots which, once they reach the ground, become prop roots to support the limbs. Fruit are red, or sometimes yellow, and are about ⅓ inch in diameter. This tree may grow to 90 feet with a crown spread of 50 feet.

WHERE DID THEY COME FROM? WHERE HAVE THEY SPREAD?

All three of these fig trees are native to the Old World, principally Southeast Asia, and were introduced into Florida in 1928-29. Figs are pollinated by minuscule "fig wasps" that spend most of their lives in a symbiotic relationship with their host trees. Each wasp

TREES

Lofty fig *(F. altissima)* and its cousins have invaded pine rockland and hardwood forest ecosystems throughout southern Florida.

species is an effective pollinator of just one or two fig species. Many New and Old World non-native fig species are cultivated in southern Florida, but without their pollinating wasps have never been capable of producing viable seeds. Sometime in recent years the pollinating wasps of these three fig species were inadvertently imported into southern Florida on either cargo ships or aircraft and the trees now produce viable seeds. The fruits are eaten and distributed by birds, and all three species have invaded pine rockland and hardwood forest ecosystems.

continues on the next page

TREES

Banyan fig, like lofty and laurel figs, often grows as an epiphyte on a host tree. The figs' constricting roots, the shade they create and the competition for nutrients eventually kill their hosts.

continued from the preceding page

WHAT PROBLEMS DO THEY CAUSE?
Seeds of these species tend to germinate in the crotches of other trees, growing as epiphytes on their host tree until aerial roots reach the ground. Like the Florida native strangler fig, *Ficus aurea*, the combination of these figs' constricting roots, shade and competition for nutrients usually kills the host tree. They are also becoming increasingly visible growing in cracks in concrete, especially on turnpike overpasses, bridges, walls, buildings and other concrete or stone structures, and if left unchecked, the roots of these trees will cause extensive structural damage and can buckle roadways.

These figs grow to immense proportions and have the potential to compete heavily with native plants for sunlight, nutrients and space in natural forest communities.

HOW CAN THEY BE CONTROLLED?
Fig trees are particularly sensitive to triclopyr herbicides as a basal or cut-stump treatment. Trees found growing on concrete or rock structures should be treated with herbicide while young to avoid costly structural damage. Use extreme caution when applying herbicide to figs growing as epiphytes to ensure that the poison does not contact the host tree. When exotic figs germinate high in the branches of large trees in natural forest communities, it may be extraordinarily difficult to get close enough to the fig to treat it.

None of these three fig species should be planted within parks or along roadways near natural forest communities in southern Florida. All three are currently on the prohibited list of landscape plants in Dade County, Florida.

Roger L. Hammer, Metropolitan Dade County Park and Recreation Department

TREES

WHAT DOES IT LOOK LIKE?

This is the familiar deciduous fig tree that produces edible fruit. Mature trees often have multiple trunks and may grow to 30 feet tall. The heavy trunk and branches have smooth, light gray, flaky bark. Leaves are bright green and have the classic fig-leaf shape, with three to five lobes. While fruit color varies in cultivated varieties, those growing wild usually produce greenish yellow fruits. Two "crops" of fruit are produced each year, however, one in the late spring and a second somewhat larger crop in late summer.

Fig trees have invaded California's Central Valley and southern coast.

WHERE DID IT COME FROM? WHERE HAS IT SPREAD?

The edible fig is native to the Mediterranean region of Europe, western Asia and north Africa. It has invaded streamside forests and other riparian habitats, and canal banks in and around California's Central Valley, southern coast and Channel Islands.

WHAT PROBLEMS DOES IT CAUSE?

The trees grow very quickly and spread vegetatively, forming dense thickets. If not controlled they can crowd out the native trees and understory shrubs characteristic of California's riparian forests, which are already rare.

HOW CAN IT BE CONTROLLED?

Young figs hand-pull fairly easily, and a small or medium weed wrench can help remove some of the larger saplings. Trees resprout vigorously after cutting but repeated cutting of resprouts may eventually exhaust the root reserves of a tree or small thicket if the interval between cuttings is short enough (four to six weeks). Edible fig is difficult to control without herbicides. Land managers have had some success cutting all trunks and sucker shoots in a thicket 6 to 18 inches above the ground and applying a triclopyr herbicide to the stumps several years in a row. The herbicide can also be applied in a 8- to 12-inch wide band around the uncut trunks of smaller trees with trunk diameters up to 2 or 3 inches.

John M. Randall, The Nature Conservancy, Davis, California

In the past 30 years, stands of melaleuca have exploded in freshwater wetlands in south Florida.

WHAT DOES IT LOOK LIKE?

Melaleuca grows to 50 feet or more. It has thick, spongy, white bark and lance-shaped leaves that smell like camphor when crushed. White flowers are borne in bottlebrush-like spikes along the stems, as are tightly packed clusters of woody seed capsules.

WHERE DID IT COME FROM? WHERE HAS IT SPREAD?

A native of northern Australia and New Guinea, melaleuca was introduced to the southern portions of the U.S. around 1900 as an ornamental tree needing little or no care. Over the last three decades, prolific seed production, adaptation to fire, tolerance of flooding and the lack of natural competitors or predators have enabled it to undergo an explosive invasion of freshwater wetlands in southern Florida.

WHAT PROBLEMS DOES IT CAUSE?

Melaleuca rapidly colonizes freshwater wetlands and almost completely displaces native wetland vegetation, degrading prime wildlife habitat. It is a major pest in the Big Cypress National Preserve and to the northern portions of the Everglades. Its flowers and new foliage produce volatile emanations that cause serious asthma-like problems or a fine, burning rash coupled with headache and nausea in sensitive people.

HOW CAN IT BE CONTROLLED?

Seedlings and saplings can be hand-pulled and larger trees cut, but follow-up control measures are necessary to prevent reinvasion and resprouting from seeds, stumps and fallen trunks. Seed capsules must be removed and destroyed. In remote areas, cut stumps are treated with a wetland-approved imazapyr herbicide mixed 20 percent with water. Trees can also be girdled with a chainsaw and the cut area treated with imazapyr diluted 50 percent with water. Basally applied herbicides are not effective. Prescribed fire during the dry season is another effective management tool to control seedlings in wetlands. However, adult trees will release huge numbers of seeds following a fire and these can quickly establish on moist soil and grow into dense thickets.

Roger L. Hammer, Metropolitan Dade County Park and Recreation Department

Chinaberry tree now grows prolifically throughout the Southeast. In Florida the plant has had such a disruptive effect on native plant communities that it's listed as a Category I invasive by the Florida Exotic Pest Plant Council, and four counties have banned its use.

WHAT DOES IT LOOK LIKE?

Chinaberry tree can grow to 40 feet tall and has lacy, bipinnate, deciduous, dark green foliage with a characteristic musky odor. In summer, it has attractive 8-inch blue blossoms followed by sticky yellow fruits.

WHERE DID IT COME FROM? WHERE HAS IT SPREAD?

A native of southwestern Asia, the plant was initially introduced into Georgia and South Carolina around 1830 and grows prolifically in all of the southeastern states. In Florida the plant has become so widespread and is considered such a nuisance that the Florida Exotic Pest Plant Council has listed it as a Category 1 invasive plant, meaning it is a widespread species that has disrupted native plant communities.

WHAT PROBLEMS DOES IT CAUSE?

As a result of strict current quarantine/sterilization regulations governing plants introduced into the U.S., the suite of insect fauna associated with this plant in its native range—as with most other invasive exotic species—is not present here. Without these insects and pathogens to keep the plant in check, it has expanded its distribution at a phenomenal rate, outcompeting native upland herbaceous and deciduous plant species in open and wooded habitats from the Carolinas to Texas. In Florida alone, four counties have banned its sale, possession and cultivation.

HOW CAN IT BE CONTROLLED?

Seed production by the Chinaberry tree is phenomenal; seedlings can be hand-pulled but the preferred method of long-term control is removal of the seed-producing tree, typically with the systemic herbicide triclopyr. It is quite effective.

Greg Jubinsky, Florida Department of Environmental Protection, Tallahassee

Princess tree is most invasive in the mid-Atlantic region and Southeast, where it often outcompetes natives.

WHAT DOES IT LOOK LIKE?

The princess tree grows up to 60 feet tall. Its deciduous, heart-shaped leaves are about 15 inches long, but may be twice that on sprouts from cut stumps. The large, fragrant, lavender flowers grow in upright clusters followed by round seed pods, which remain on the tree all winter. A single tree is capable of producing 20 million seeds.

WHERE DID IT COME FROM? WHERE HAS IT SPREAD?

The princess tree, native to China, was introduced to Europe in the 1830s and to North America a few years later. Initially used as an ornamental, it has escaped cultivation in the eastern half of the U.S. In warm regions it can grow in almost any habitat and is often seen in vacant lots. It is of most concern in the mid-Atlantic region and Southeast.

WHAT PROBLEMS DOES IT CAUSE?

Princess tree outcompetes natives from Pennsylvania and Georgia west to Missouri. Seedlings colonize rocky cliffs and sandy stream banks, quickly invading after disturbances such as fire, construction, gypsy moth defoliation or floods. The trees also cause maintenance problems along roads and utility rights-of-way and in gardens.

HOW CAN IT BE CONTROLLED?

Small seedlings can be hand-pulled, but remove all parts of the roots. Larger trees can be cut or girdled, but resprouts are common. Repeated cutting will eventually exhaust the roots; with large trees this may take several years. Treat cut stumps immediately with a 50 percent solution of glyphosate or triclopyr herbicide to prevent sprouting. On small trees a foliar application of 2 percent glyphosate is effective.

Kristine Johnson, Great Smoky Mountains National Park, Tennessee

WHAT DOES IT LOOK LIKE?

White poplar is a fast-growing tree reaching 70 to 90 feet at maturity. Leaves are roughly triangular, typically with three to five and sometimes seven lobes. The leaves are coarsely toothed and have hairy white undersides. Seeds of white poplar have long, silky white hairs.

WHERE DID IT COME FROM? WHERE HAS IT SPREAD?

White poplar is native to western and central Eurasia and northern Africa. It was brought to North America early in the Colonial era and was planted as a landscape and street tree, on farms and in cities, and has spread from these original plantings. It has since escaped cultivation and reproduces on its own throughout North America.

WHAT PROBLEMS DOES IT CAUSE?

White poplar primarily invades grasslands and open areas. Although it was often planted because it grows rapidly, it is a poor choice for a landscape tree. It reproduces rapidly and vegetatively by sending out suckers that arise from the roots of the "mother" tree, and continual cutting of the suckers is necessary to keep it from shading and crowding out native and desirable vegetation. The water-hungry roots can clog sewers and drainpipes, and its soft wood is susceptible to storm damage and many diseases. White poplar drops its twigs and limbs throughout the year, leaving yards messy with debris.

TREES

White poplar, first planted as a street and landscape tree on farms and in cities, reproduces rapidly and vegetatively by sending out suckers that arise from the roots of the "mother" tree. It has since escaped cultivation and now grows in the wild throughout North America.

HOW CAN IT BE CONTROLLED?

Control existing trees and suckers with frequent cutting, preferably from June through August. It can take years of cutting all stems and the trunk to kill the "mother" plant. An herbicide such as glyphosate can be used as a foliar spray or cut-surface treatment (treat each and every stem). Several applications over many years may be needed to kill the plant.

William Glass, Illinois Department of Natural Resources

TREES

Black locust, an eastern North American native, now invades disturbed woodlands of urban and rural landscapes throughout the continent.

WHAT DOES IT LOOK LIKE?

Black locust is a deciduous tree with an open crown that grows to 80 feet tall. Its bark is deeply furrowed, branches usually have spines, and the compound leaves are 8 to 12 inches long with seven to 19 rounded leaflets. White pea-like flowers, borne May to June on inflorescences from the current year's growth, develop into reddish pods 3 to 4 inches long.

WHERE DID IT COME FROM? WHERE HAS IT SPREAD?

Black locust is a native of eastern North America from Pennsylvania and southern Indiana south to Georgia and Louisiana, and west to Iowa, Missouri and Oklahoma. Because of its useful wood, nitrogen-fixing ability and attractive flowers, it has been planted widely beyond this original range and now grows in the wild throughout the U.S. and southern Canada. While intolerant of shade or poorly drained soils, it occurs in many habitats—in the East in disturbed woodlands and forests of urban and agricultural landscapes. In the West, its distribution is more restricted, and it is typically found on heavily disturbed lands such as roadsides, and in stream bottoms and ravines. It has also escaped from cultivation in the Northeast and upper Midwest.

WHAT PROBLEMS DOES IT CAUSE?

Through root sprouts and seeds, black locust creates stands of considerable size. Outside of black locust's original range, these stands displace native vegetation in woodlands and pinelands and riparian areas in the eastern portions of the nation and in riparian areas including along desert watercourses in the far West. Its seeds, leaves and bark are toxic to humans and livestock.

HOW CAN IT BE CONTROLLED?

Black locust resprouts vigorously from stump and roots when cut. Repeated (and persistent) cutting of these sprouts can kill the tree. More effective control can be obtained by brushing the freshly cut stump with a full-strength glyphosate herbicide.

John Hunter, Dept. of Biological Sciences, State University of New York, Brockport

TREES

WHAT DOES IT LOOK LIKE?

This small to medium-sized tree has deciduous heart-shaped leaves and is prized for its bright display of fall foliage followed by bundles of waxy white seeds, which have inspired the nickname, "popcorn tree." The three-lobed fruit clings to the tree throughout the winter or at least until "harvested" by migrating birds.

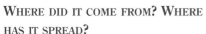

First introduced into the U.S. by Ben Franklin, Chinese tallow tree is invasive along the Gulf Coast from Corpus Christi to Florida and up the East Coast to North Carolina.

WHERE DID IT COME FROM? WHERE HAS IT SPREAD?

Tallow tree is native to China where it has been cultivated for the last 14 centuries as a seed oil crop. First introduced into the U.S. by Ben Franklin in 1776, it has become recognized as an invasive plant along the Gulf Coast from Corpus Christi to Florida and up the East Coast to North Carolina. The primary vector for spread appears to be migrating birds that gorge themselves on the seed. The average tallow tree yields approximately 100,000 seeds per year and viability approaches 85 percent.

WHAT PROBLEMS DOES IT CAUSE?

Tallow tree typically grows in wetlands, swamps and bottomland forests, readily outcompeting native hardwoods such as cypress, tupelo, black gum and willow, thereby decreasing native plant diversity and ultimately having a negative effect on wildlife.

HOW CAN IT BE CONTROLLED?

Hand-pulling of seedlings is effective, but cutting trees older than one year results in root and stump suckering. Resource managers have found that the only effective way to control this invasive weed is to apply a systemic herbicide such as triclopyr to the base of the tree.

Greg Jubinsky, Florida Department of Environmental Protection, Tallahassee

TREES

In tropical and warm temperate regions, umbrella tree invades hardwood forests and margins, roadsides and cultivated grounds.

WHAT DOES IT LOOK LIKE?

This tree is easily recognized by its unusual palm-like leaves with seven to 16 large leaflets that radiate outward from the tip of the elongated leaf stem, forming a leafy umbrella. Long sprays of bright red flowers extend outward in different directions from a common point at the tip of each branch and stand out above the foliage. Small, round, purplish red fruit are produced in great numbers on mature trees.

WHERE DID IT COME FROM? WHERE HAS IT SPREAD?

A native of Australia, umbrella tree is a popular landscape tree in southern Florida, and a favorite indoor plant in colder regions. In tropical and warm temperate regions, where it is grown outdoors, it readily escapes cultivation, invading undisturbed hardwood forests, forest margins, roadsides and cultivated grounds. Birds distribute the seeds to new areas.

WHAT PROBLEMS DOES IT CAUSE?

Once established, umbrella tree quickly forms dense thickets in southern Florida, competing with native plants for light, space and nutrients. Seeds often germinate in the old leaf bases of palms or in the crotches of large trees, growing as epiphytes until roots reach the ground.

HOW CAN IT BE CONTROLLED?

Pull seedlings and young saplings by hand. Older trees can be controlled with a basal application of a triclopyr herbicide mixed with an oil diluent. Or you can cut the tree down and treat the stump with a triclopyr herbicide mixed 50 percent with water. When this tree grows epiphytically, make sure that herbicide does not come in contact with the host tree. It may take months for the herbicide to take effect and follow-up treatments may be required.

Roger L. Hammer, Metropolitan Dade County Park and Recreation Department

Tamarix ramosissima, T. chinensis, T. parviflora Tamarisk

WHAT DO THEY LOOK LIKE?

Tamarisks are tall shrubs or small trees commonly found alongside rivers throughout the arid and semiarid West. They frequently grow across large areas in dense, impenetrable tangles of stems up to 30 feet tall. Tamarisks look somewhat like cedars, with minute, scaly leaves that tightly cover the branches. However, unlike cedars they produce plumes of white to pink flowers from early spring until late fall. The individual florets are small; those of *T. ramosissima* and *T. chinensis* have five petals, and those of *T. parviflora* have four petals. All three of the above tamarisk species are deciduous and similar in overall appearance, distribution and degree of invasiveness.

Tamarisk has invaded the banks of waterways in every western state but Washington and North Dakota.

WHERE DID THEY COME FROM?
WHERE HAVE THEY SPREAD?

Tamarisks are native to the Mediterranean region eastward across the Middle East to China and Japan. They were imported into the U.S. in the early 1800s. Although primarily used as ornamentals, tamarisks also were planted along watercourses to control erosion. At the turn of the century, the plants escaped cultivation and slowly began spreading along southwestern rivers. After 1920, the expansion surged, and major infestations developed along the Gila River in Arizona and the Pecos River and Rio Grande in New Mexico. By 1988, tamarisk had infested approximately 1,016,720 acres. Tamarisk is now prevalent in all western states except Washington and North Dakota; the states with the greatest infestations (in order) are Texas, Arizona, Utah, New Mexico and Oklahoma, and it is spreading rapidly in California. Tamarisk primarily inhabits areas where its roots can reach groundwater and the plant can tolerate saline conditions by exuding salt from its leaves.

WHAT PROBLEMS DO THEY CAUSE?

Tamarisk decreases biological diversi-
continues on the next page

43

Tamarisk displaces native streamside vegetation, providing food that few species of native wildlife can use and increasing sediment deposition.

continued from the preceding page
ty by displacing native riparian (streamside) vegetation and by providing a food source that few species of native riparian wildlife can use. Tamarisk growth chokes drainages, increasing sediment deposition and the likelihood and severity of floods. Wildfires are more frequent in areas dominated by tamarisk; the fires kill many native riparian plants whereas the tamarisk quickly resprouts. Tamarisk leaf litter can increase soil salinity. Tamarisk also is considered a water-waster; its consumption of water can dry up desert oases vital to wildlife by lowering the water table.

HOW CAN THEY BE CONTROLLED?
Small seedlings can be pulled out by hand. Once established, tamarisk is difficult to control. It also can rapidly resprout from below ground, requiring the use of a systemic herbicide that is transported to the roots. The cut-stump method of herbicide application has frequently been used in riparian restoration projects to control established stands: each tamarisk is cut down and a systemic herbicide is sprayed onto the top and sides of the remaining stump.

William Wiesenborn, Bureau of Reclamation, Boulder City, Nevada

Invasions of Siberian elm have been observed from Utah and Idaho eastward.

TREES

WHAT DOES IT LOOK LIKE?

Siberian elm is a fast-growing, small to medium-sized tree with an open, round crown of slender, spreading branches. The bark is gray or brown with shallow furrows at maturity. This elm is distinguished by its smooth, elliptical, singly toothed leaves from ⅛ to 2½ inches long. Flowers are greenish, lack petals and appear in small, drooping clusters of two to five before the leaves begin to unfold in the spring. The winged fruits are one-seeded, smooth, about half an inch wide and hang in clusters.

WHERE DID IT COME FROM? WHERE HAS IT SPREAD?

Native to northern China and eastern Siberia, Siberian elm was introduced in the 1860s. It has since escaped cultivation and invasions are reported from Utah and Idaho and eastward. Because it tolerates a variety of conditions, it occurs in both dry areas and moist soils along streambanks, in pastures and prairies and along roadsides.

WHAT PROBLEMS DOES IT CAUSE?

Seeds disseminated by the wind form thickets of hundreds of seedlings. Initial growth is fast. Older trees lose branches, become messy and lose ornamental appeal. Siberian elm can invade and in a few years dominate prairies, particularly if they have been subject to past disturbance.

HOW CAN IT BE CONTROLLED?

Hand-pull seedlings. Girdle large trees in late spring to mid-summer when sap is flowing and the bark peels away from the sapwood. Don't girdle too deeply or the tree will resprout from the roots. Girdled trees die slowly over one to two years. Trees can also be cut and stumps treated with a glyphosate herbicide to prevent resprouting. Regular burning should control Siberian elm in fire-adapted plant communities such as prairies.

Jill Kennay, Natural Land Institute, Rockford, Illinois

SHRUBS

Shoebutton ardisia has become a serious invasive weed in hardwood forests and on abandoned agricultural land within Everglades National Park and throughout southern Florida, forming dense stands that crowd out native plant species.

WHAT DOES IT LOOK LIKE?

Shoebutton ardisia is a shrub or small tree with leathery, lance-shaped leaves that grow singly at different heights and on different sides of the stem. The new growth is rose-pink. Five-petaled rose-colored flowers, borne in clusters, are produced throughout the year, as are rounded black fruits, but peak flowering is generally in the summer.

WHERE DID IT COME FROM? WHERE HAS IT SPREAD?

A native of India, shoebutton ardisia has escaped cultivation in southern Florida and become a serious invasive weed in hardwood forests and on abandoned agricultural land within Everglades National Park.

WHAT PROBLEMS DOES IT CAUSE?

The fruits of cultivated plants are distributed by birds and quickly invade nearby hardwood forests. Once established shoebutton ardisia forms dense, virtual single-species stands in the forest understory, crowding out native plant species. It can be mistaken for the closely related native marlberry, *Ardisia escallonioides*, but shoebutton ardisia produces clusters of flowers and fruit at the axil while marlberry bears flowers and fruit at branch tips.

HOW CAN IT BE CONTROLLED?

Seedlings can be hand-pulled in areas where the soil is already disturbed or on other sites where disturbing the soil won't cause problems. Soil disturbance in natural areas, especially pine rockland habitat, invites further invasion by exotic plants. In areas with a dense groundcover of seedlings, a broadcast spray of a glyphosate herbicide is effective, but be careful to avoid damaging desirable plants. Mature specimens should be treated with a basal application of a triclopyr herbicide mixed with an oil diluent.

Roger L. Hammer, Metropolitan Dade County Park and Recreation Department

WHAT DOES IT LOOK LIKE?

Barberry is a deciduous shrub with dense foliage that grows 3 to 6 feet tall. The leaves are small and rounded and vary in color by cultivar. The shrub is most easily recognized by its short spines and the bright red berries that develop in late summer.

WHERE DID IT COME FROM? WHERE HAS IT SPREAD?

Native to Asia, Japanese barberry was first cultivated in the U.S. in the late 1800s. It now grows in the wild along roadsides and thickets, particularly in the East and Midwest. In New Jersey, Connecticut and New York, where it has become extremely invasive in recent years, it is invading old fields and early successional woodlands.

SHRUBS

Japanese barberry has become extremely invasive in New Jersey, Connecticut and New York in recent years, and is also a problem throughout the East and Midwest.

WHAT PROBLEMS DOES IT CAUSE?

Japanese barberry grows equally well in full sun or partial shade and adapts to nearly any soil type. It is a particular threat to open, second-growth forests. Once established, it can become so thick that it shades out other understory species, with possible adverse effects on birds and other wildlife that depend on native plant species.

HOW CAN IT BE CONTROLLED?

Control Japanese barberry by hand-pulling or digging early in the season before seed set. Remove as much of the root system as possible because it will resprout. Although it has shallow roots, it is tough to get it out of the ground because of the stiff spines; wear thick, heavy gloves. When digging would disturb the soil too much, cut the shrub at the base in the winter or spring. If it resprouts, treat with an herbicide such as glyphosate. Once removed from old field habitats, regular mowing may prevent re-establishment of the shrub. In Midwest oak savannahs, prescribed fire has successfully reduced populations.

Elizabeth Johnson, The Nature Conservancy, New Jersey

SHRUBS

Butterfly bush has escaped cultivation along the eastern seaboard from Pennsylvania to North Carolina, and in California, Oregon and Washington, colonizing roadsides and riparian (streamside) zones.

WHERE DID IT COME FROM? WHERE HAS IT SPREAD?

Originally from China, it has been grown in the U.S. since about 1900 and has escaped from cultivation along the eastern seaboard from Pennsylvania to North Carolina, and along the West Coast in California, Oregon and Washington. It generally colonizes disturbed areas such as roadsides and riparian zones. Other members of this genus (for example, *B. madagascarensis, B. lindleyana,* and *B. asiatica*) have also shown strong invasive ability while others (such as *B. globosa*) have not. Therefore, unidentified members of this genus should be observed and removed from the garden if they show signs of spreading.

WHAT PROBLEMS DOES IT CAUSE?

Butterfly bush does not yet present a serious problem but is spreading rapidly.

HOW CAN IT BE CONTROLLED?

The species does not vegetatively reproduce via underground parts, so it is fairly easy to remove established plants. Be sure to remove the stump or treat it with a glyphosate herbicide, as the plant can regenerate from the roots if cut.

Sarah Reichard, Department of Zoology, University of Washington, Seattle

WHAT DOES IT LOOK LIKE?

Butterfly bush is sometimes called the "summer lilac" because its fragrant flowers look a lot like those of lilacs and because it flowers in midsummer rather than spring. The flowers are small and usually purple with an orange center and are a nectar source for butterflies. Many cultivars with flowers in various shades of pink and purple are available. The shrub is often rangy in habit and grows up to 15 feet tall. The velvety gray-green leaves are deciduous and often fuzzy underneath.

WHAT DO THEY LOOK LIKE?

Cotoneasters are grown for their abundant clusters of red or coral berries, which line the arching branches. The berries cover the shrubs through autumn and winter. In summer they bear a profusion of tiny (¼-inch wide), white, rose-like flowers. When in flower, the shrubs are abuzz with yellow jackets. They flower and fruit best in poor, dry soils. In cold-winter areas, leaves of some species turn brilliant colors.

C. microphyllus, rockspray cotoneaster, is prostrate and densely branched. Branches are trailing and rooting, with secondary branches erect, arching and clothed with ¼-inch wide leaves. *C. lacteus* and *C. pannosus* are upright shrubs eventually exceeding 10 feet in height. The former has handsome 3-inch leaves that are shiny dark green above and densely hairy beneath, and has branches clear to the ground. *C. pannosus* is fountain-shaped, with ¾-inch leaves that are dull green above and felty underneath. Although cotoneasters are apomictic—that is, they can set seed without benefit of pollination and subsequent fertilization—they can also produce seed following pollination, and different species may hybridize. This same phenomenon occasionally makes wildland seedlings difficult to identify. Other species in addition to the three listed above may become pests.

Rockspray cotoneaster *(C. microphyllus)* and its relatives have been seen in increasing numbers in wildlands along the foggy central and northern California coast.

WHERE DID THEY COME FROM?
WHERE HAVE THEY SPREAD?

Cotoneasters are native to Eurasia, principally China. They were much collected by English plant hunters, and from England made their way to U.S. gardens. Rock spray cotoneaster was introduced to England in 1824 and to California in 1854. Collectors sent additional species throughout the next century, and by 1900 a wide selection was available. For a long time they were

continues on the next page

SHRUBS

In California, cotoneasters including *C. lacteus* (left), may compete directly with the closely related native toyon *(Heteromeles arbutifolia)*, their equal in beauty.

SHRUBS

continued from the preceding page
not reported as escaping cultivation, but during the past two or three decades increasing numbers have been seen in wildlands along the foggy central and northern California coast, and they are now beginning to be taken seriously by those concerned with the health of native biological communities.

WHAT PROBLEMS DO THEY CAUSE?
Although they are still not seen in large numbers, the fact that cotoneasters are bird-distributed, can penetrate intact and seemingly healthy ecosystems and thrive in poor, thin and droughty soils that many native California species claim as their domain, makes them cause for concern. All cotoneasters have aggressive root systems, and the plants shade and smother sun-loving natives. Eventually, diverse native communities are displaced by cotoneaster. In California, cotoneasters may directly compete with the closely related native toyon (*Heteromeles arbutifolia*), its equal in beauty.

HOW CAN THEY BE CONTROLLED?
Although they have a tough and deep root system, while young they can be uprooted with a weed wrench. Because cotoneasters branch profusely at ground level, this technique cannot be used on larger plants. Cutting branches to the stump and painting them with a 100 percent glyphosate herbicide is very effective. The myriad seedlings surrounding cut shrubs can be either smothered with mulch or black plastic, hand-pulled or sprayed.

Jake Sigg, California Native Plant Society, San Francisco

WHAT DOES IT LOOK LIKE?
Singleseed hawthorn is a tall deciduous shrub or small tree in the rose family. The leaves are small and divided into three to seven lobes, and grow singly at different heights and on different sides of the stems. The twigs have medium-sized spines. Clusters of fragrant white flowers (sometimes fading to pale pink) appear in spring, followed in the fall by an abundant crop of small red fruits.

WHERE DID IT COME FROM? WHERE HAS IT SPREAD?
Native to Europe, singleseed hawthorn was introduced into North America as a garden ornamental. Birds and other wildlife eat the fruits, spreading the species from gardens into the wild. This hawthorn has also been planted around the edges of pastures to form "living fences." It is tolerant of both shade and sun and grows in woodlands, hedgerows, meadows and in other natural and semi-natural habitats in the Pacific Northwest.

WHAT PROBLEMS DOES IT CAUSE?
A prolific seed producer, singleseed hawthorn can eventually form dense thickets that exclude virtually all understory plants. It grows and can hybridize with native hawthorn species such as black hawthorn *(C. douglasii)*. These hybrids may contaminate the gene pool of the native species.

SHRUBS

Singleseed hawthorn invades woodlands, hedgerows, meadows and other natural habitats in the Pacific Northwest. This prolific seed producer can, over time, form dense thickets that exclude virtually all understory plants.

HOW CAN IT BE CONTROLLED?
The best way to control the spread of singleseed hawthorn is to eliminate seed sources; this is difficult to achieve once a population is well established. Smaller seedlings can be pulled or dug up. Larger individuals can be cut, but they will resprout from the cut stumps unless painted with a glyphosate herbicide.

Edward R. Alverson, The Nature Conservancy, Willamette Valley, Oregon

SHRUBS

Scotch broom covers more than 2 million acres in Washington, Oregon and California.

WHAT DOES IT LOOK LIKE?

Scotch broom is a leguminous, upright shrub 6 to 9 feet tall. Young branches generally have five green ridges with hairs on them; as they mature the hairs fall off and the branches become tan and lose the distinct ridges. In late March to early May, the shrub is covered with a profusion of golden yellow pea-like flowers.

WHERE DID IT COME FROM? WHERE HAS IT SPREAD?

Native to Europe and North Africa, Scotch broom was introduced in the 1850s as an ornamental and later used to prevent erosion and stabilize dunes. It currently occupies more than 2 million acres in Washington, Oregon and coastal and Sierra Nevada foothill regions of California. It also infests large areas in southwestern British Columbia, and a few small areas along the U.S. Atlantic seaboard. It colonizes grasslands, shrublands and open canopy forest.

WHAT PROBLEMS DOES IT CAUSE?

Scotch broom spreads via prodigious production of long-lived seeds, and can also resprout from the root crown. It displaces native plant species and animal forage species, and makes reforestation difficult. Broom is flammable and carries fire to the tree canopy layer where fires burn hotter and are more destructive. In nitrogen-poor soils it is very competitive because of the nitrogen-fixing bacteria in the root nodules.

HOW CAN IT BE CONTROLLED?

Remove mature broom with a weed-pulling tool or brush hog machine; saw-cutting the stems encourages resprouting unless done near the ground in the dry season. Mechanical control works best on isolated shrubs and small patches. The most effective chemical control is a 25 percent triclopyr herbicide in 75 percent oil surfactant applied in a band around the lower portion of the trunk just after flowering. Prescribed burning helps deplete the seedbank but must be repeated two and four years later. After older plants are removed, emerging seedlings are likely to appear for at least five years and must be hand-pulled, weed whipped, herbicided or burned.

Carla Bossard, Department of Biology, St. Mary's College of California

Russian olive tolerates drought and poor soils, making it a popular landscaping choice in the West, where it has escaped cultivation in 17 states. It takes over streambanks, lake shores and wet meadows, choking out native cottonwoods and willows.

SHRUBS

WHAT DOES IT LOOK LIKE?

Russian olive is a large deciduous shrub that can grow to over 25 feet tall. It has distinctive silver-gray leaves, woody thorns and smooth, reddish brown bark. Small clusters of aromatic yellow flowers bloom in late spring, followed by hard, olive-shaped fruits.

WHERE DID IT COME FROM? WHERE HAS IT SPREAD?

Native to Europe and western Asia, Russian olive was brought to North America in the early 1900s. Since the great droughts of the 1930s, it has been promoted for windbreaks, erosion control and wildlife habitat enhancement. Tolerance of drought and poor soils make it popular for landscaping in the West, where it has escaped cultivation in 17 states and continues to spread.

WHAT PROBLEMS DOES IT CAUSE?

Russian olives quickly take over streambanks, lake shores and wet meadows, choking out native vegetation, such as cottonwoods and willows, which are unable to regenerate. Birds who rely on the insects and nesting cavities in cottonwoods and willows are adversely affected. It is particularly troublesome in the Intermountain West and western Plains.

HOW CAN IT BE CONTROLLED?

Control is difficult once trees mature. Any control should be undertaken before fruiting to prevent the spread of seeds. Trees smaller than 4 inches in diameter should be pulled out with a weed-pulling tool when the ground is moist. Larger trees should be cut down to ground level. The stump should be completely buried or an appropriate herbicide should immediately be applied to the cut surface. Watch for resprouting on the root lines the following growing season. Girdling, stump burning and depositing rock salt inside holes drilled into the stump may have limited success.

Laurie Deiter, City of Boulder Open Space Department, Colorado

Autumn olive is most problematic in the Midwest, Northeast and Southeast, growing rapidly into an impenetrable, thorny thicket and usurping space from native species.

WHAT DOES IT LOOK LIKE?

Autumn olive is a shrub up to 20 feet tall, with fragrant yellow flowers that emerge after the leaves in spring and mature into bunches of red fruits in early fall. It frequently is thorny, with sharp spur branches that can reach several inches in length. It has distinctive gray-green leaves that are shorter and less silvery than those of Russian olive.

WHERE DID IT COME FROM? WHERE HAS IT SPREAD?

It was introduced into North America in 1917 from mountain streambank and thicket habitats from Afghanistan east to China, Korea and Japan. The shrub can dominate almost any landscape type, from fencerows to meadows to open woods, even sand dunes and mine spoils. It is limited by lack of reliable hardiness from USDA zone 5 north, but still can escape there to become a pest. The plant is most problematic in the Midwest, Northeast and Southeast.

WHAT PROBLEMS DOES IT CAUSE?

Autumn olive grows rapidly into an impenetrable, thorny thicket, usurping space from more valuable species. A single plant can produce 200,000 seeds each year, which are spread widely by birds.

HOW CAN IT BE CONTROLLED?

Pull young seedlings in early spring; it leafs out before most other shrubs and is easy to spot. Eradication of an established thicket can be difficult and expensive. On large open areas like pastures, bulldozing or aerial herbicide applications may be necessary. Where it has not yet become so dense as to prohibit entry into the stand, manual herbicide spraying can be effective, but follow-up applications almost always are required. The seed source should be located and destroyed for long-term control. Unfortunately, periodic fires, cutting or competition from native species do not reliably control autumn olive.

Guy Sternberg, Illinois Native Plant Society

WHAT DOES IT LOOK LIKE?

A deciduous shrub that may reach 12 feet tall, winged euonymus forms a broad, closed crown. The green twigs have four wide, corky wings, which easily distinguish winged euonymus from most other species. The elliptical leaves are usually less than 2 inches long, have toothed margins and turn a bright scarlet to purplish red in autumn—hence the name burning bush. The small yellow-green flowers are not obvious, but the smooth purplish fruits add color in late summer.

WHERE DID IT COME FROM? WHERE HAS IT SPREAD?

A native of northeast Asia, winged euonymus was introduced into the U.S. in the 1860s. It grows well in full sun to nearly full shade and in dry to relatively moist soils. It is used in foundation plantings and as hedges and is commonly planted along interstate highways. Many cultivars are available. In the past 30 years this species has escaped from cultivation in the eastern United States.

WHAT PROBLEMS DOES IT CAUSE?

In some woodland habitats, winged euonymus is replacing native shrubs. It is most problematic in open woods but also, according to recent reports, in mature second-growth upland forests and pastures and hill prairies in the East and Midwest. Disseminated by birds,

SHRUBS

Winged euonymus has escaped cultivation in the eastern U.S. and Midwest. It's most problematic in open woods, mature second-growth forests and pastures.

seedlings are common throughout woods and hill prairies where ornamental plantings are nearby.

HOW CAN IT BE CONTROLLED?

Winged euonymus can be controlled by cutting and painting the stumps with a glyphosate herbicide. Foliar spraying with a glyphosate herbicide in early summer may be necessary where large populations have become established.

John E. Ebinger, Botany Department, Eastern Illinois University

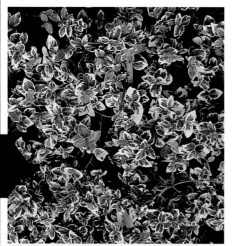

SHRUBS

Wintercreeper, also called climbing euonymus, has spread into forests and rocky bluffs in the East and Midwest from Chicago south.

WHAT DOES IT LOOK LIKE?

Wintercreeper is an evergreen climbing shrub with leathery leaves opposite each other on the stem. Wintercreeper spreads across the ground to form a dense groundcover or climbs up trees, rocks and buildings. It climbs by attaching to objects with numerous small roots arising from the stems. Groundcover populations seldom flower and fruit; however, climbing stems produce long-stalked clusters of four-petaled flowers in June, followed by fruits that look like smooth capsules and split open in the fall to reveal scarlet berries.

WHERE DID IT COME FROM? WHERE HAS IT SPREAD?

Wintercreeper was introduced into North America from Asia primarily for use as an evergreen groundcover. It has spread into upland and lowland forests and rocky bluffs in the eastern and midwestern states from the latitude of Chicago southward. It can spread and appear many miles from the nearest planting because its fruits are eaten by birds, which disperse the seeds.

WHAT PROBLEMS DOES IT CAUSE?

Wintercreeper forms dense mats that smother and kill wildflowers, forming single-species stands. It can also smother and kill trees. The loss of landscape diversity means less food and shelter for the butterflies and many other creatures that depend on native vegetation.

HOW CAN IT BE CONTROLLED?

Light infestations can be hand-pulled, but be careful to get all of the root. Denser infestations can be eradicated by cutting the stems at ground level and carefully applying a 20 percent solution of glyphosate herbicide to the cut stem. You can control fruiting and seed-spread from existing stands by cutting all vertically climbing stems, which are generally the only ones to flower and fruit.

John E. Schwegman, Division of Natural Heritage, Illinois Department of Natural Resources

English holly is a recent invader of the Northwest, but is causing concern because it is an increasingly common sight in the now rare ancient forests of the region, where it changes the character and structure of the understory.

SHRUBS

WHAT DOES IT LOOK LIKE?

English holly is a tree or shrub usually with a conical shape. The dark, glossy, evergreen leaves are edged with sharp spines. Small, greenish white male or female flowers emerge in May and June. Clusters of bright red berries form on female plants in the fall and may persist for several months if birds don't eat them.

WHERE DID IT COME FROM? WHERE HAS IT SPREAD?

The species is native to Europe, West Africa and the Mediterranean region. It has been used in American gardens since around 1700 and in about 1869 was introduced into the Pacific Northwest, where it is being spread at an increasing rate into forests by birds that eat the fruits.

WHAT PROBLEMS DOES IT CAUSE?

The effects of English holly on native species and communities in the Northwest are unknown because of the fairly recent onset of the invasions. However, the plant is causing concern because it is increasingly appearing in the now rare ancient forests of the region. It changes the character and structure of these forests, adding a tall shrub layer that is not normally found.

HOW CAN IT BE CONTROLLED?

Fortunately, English holly is easy to remove mechanically. Because the species does not reproduce vegetatively, it can easily and cleanly be pulled out of the ground, especially when young. In Northwest forests be careful to not pull out native barberry seedlings *(Mahonia aquifolium* and *M. nervosa)* by mistake—they look similar to those of holly. Large hollies can resprout from the stump, so if cut they should be painted with a glyphosate herbicide.

Sarah Reichard, Department of Zoology, University of Washington, Seattle

SHRUBS

Chinese privet, like its related species, is problematic throughout the East and is extremely aggressive, forming dense, impenetrable thickets that crowd out more desirable plants.

WHAT DO THEY LOOK LIKE?
The genus *Ligustrum* includes several species that have escaped from cultivation. Three troublesome species are common or European privet, Chinese privet and Japanese privet. The three species are similar in appearance. All three species were introduced as garden plants and have been used widely as hedges. In addition, all three produce black, berry-like fruits, which often persist into early spring.

L. vulgare, common or European privet, is a stout, many-branched, deciduous shrub that grows to 15 feet tall. The leaves have short stalks, are smooth underneath and grow opposite each other on the stem. Clusters of small, white flowers are produced from May through June.

L. sinense, Chinese privet, also grows to 15 feet tall. It has evergreen to semi-evergreen leaves that are hairy on the midrib underneath and grow opposite each other on the stem. The twigs are also hairy. Dense clusters of small, white flowers bloom from April through June.

L. japonicum, Japanese privet, is a dense evergreen shrub that reaches 18 feet in height. The stems are squarish with large, raised lenticels, or pores. The leaves grow opposite each other on the stem, are almost a black-green color with reddish margins and

Like the other species, Japanese privet invades river bottoms, open woods, fencerows and road-sides, and is a prolific producer of seed. This species is not as hardy as Chinese and European privet, and is more of a problem in the Southeast.

SHRUBS

midrib, and are leathery in texture. Its clusters of small, white, fragrant flowers are produced from May through August.

WHERE DID THEY COME FROM? WHERE HAVE THEY SPREAD?
Common or European privet, as the name implies, is native to Europe and was introduced into the U.S. sometime in the middle of this century. Chinese privet, native to China, was introduced into this country in 1952. Japanese privet is native to Japan and Korea. It was introduced into the U.S. in 1945. These privets have escaped from cultivation and are troublesome throughout the eastern half of the U.S. Japanese privet is not as hardy as the other two species and is more of a problem in the Southeast.

WHAT PROBLEMS DO THEY CAUSE?
These three privets are extremely aggressive and can form dense, impen-etrable thickets that crowd out more desirable plants. They invade natural areas, including river bottoms, open woods, fencerows and roadsides. They are prolific producers of seed relished by birds, which can spread them far from the original planting. They also spread by suckers.

HOW CAN THEY BE CONTROLLED?
Once these privets become established, they are difficult to control. In gardens, smaller plants can be dug out. Hand removal is almost impossible with larger plants. For these, chemical control with glyphosate herbicides is most effective. Foliage treatment is best for actively growing plants and cut-stump treatment for freshly cut wood.

Patricia Dalton Haragan, Davies Herbarium, University of Louisville, Kentucky

SHRUBS

Tatarian honeysuckle now grows in a wide swath from Utah and California to Maine and southern Canada.

What do they look like?

Bush honeysuckles are upright, deciduous, multi-stemmed shrubs that can be tall and tree-like or short and densely branched, depending on species and habitat. Bush honeysuckles have dark green leaves and produce a profusion of flowers in spring, followed by an abundance of showy fruits.

Amur honeysuckle (*L. maackii*) is the tallest, reaching up to 30 feet on rich soils. It is also the most variable in growth form: in forests it becomes tall and spindly, while in sunnier habitats it is shorter and more compact. Amur honeysuckle leafs out in early spring, well before native shrubs, and drops its leaves well after theirs have fallen.

The elliptical leaves average about 2¾ inches long and taper to a relatively long, slender point. Flowers start out white, sometimes tinged with pink, and yellow with age. In fall, the berries turn glossy red. The cultivar 'Rem-Red' is often recommended for its superior fruit display.

Morrow honeysuckle (*L. morrowii*) is a dense, wide shrub that reaches about 6½ feet tall. The 1½-inch-long leaves are oval with short-pointed tips. Flowers are initially white but yellow with age. The berries, typically dark red, ripen in early summer. The cultivar 'Xanthocarpa' produces yellow or orange berries.

Tatarian honeysuckle (*L. tatarica*) is a compact shrub growing to 10 feet tall. Leaves are similar to those of Morrow honeysuckle. Depending on the cultivar, flower color ranges from pure white to red; fruits vary from yellow to dark red. Morrow honeysuckle and tatarian honeysuckle may hybridize with each other, producing *Lonicera* x *bella* (belle honeysuckle), and with other honeysuckles, making identification difficult.

Where did they come from? Where have they spread?

Amur honeysuckle is native to China, Korea and Japan, and was introduced to North America in 1896. It is now established or escaped in 24 eastern states and Ontario; invasion has been most extensive in Illinois, Indiana, Kentucky, Ohio, Tennessee and West

Virginia. Morrow honeysuckle, native to Japan, was introduced to the U.S. in the late 1800s. Today it occurs in a broad band from Wyoming to Maine and southern Canada. Tatarian honeysuckle, native to Turkey and southern Russia, was introduced by the mid-1700s and now grows in a wide swath from Utah and California to Maine and southern Canada.

Amur honeysuckle has escaped in 24 eastern states and Ontario.

SHRUBS

WHAT PROBLEMS DO THEY CAUSE?

Bush honeysuckles colonize a variety of habitats, from open (old fields, marshes, roadsides) to shaded (upland and lowland forests), but are most successful in full sun. Generally, disturbed urban forests are more readily invaded than large, intact rural ones.

Bush honeysuckles can transform prairies into scrub. In forest preserves they can reduce the plant diversity of the ground layer and decrease the density of tree seedlings, with possible long-term effects on tree populations. However, very few studies have been done to determine specifically how bush honeysuckles interact with other species in biological communities. Clearly, native birds feed on the fruits in winter and may use the shrubs for nesting.

HOW CAN THEY BE CONTROLLED?

Isolated shrubs less than 3 years of age are easy to hand-pull. Dense thickets are more problematic: removal of the shrub canopy can expose soil, making it susceptible to erosion or invasion by other invasive species, and seeds in the soil will regenerate bush honeysuckle populations. Thus, a successful control program will take several years. Adult plants in all habitats can be killed by cutting stems down to the shrub base and then painting it with a 20 percent solution of glyphosate herbicide. In shadier environments they can be killed by repeated clipping; but avoid clipping in sunny sites as it can result in even greater stem densities. After adult plants are eliminated, seedlings must be hand-pulled. Seeds in the soil are not long-lived, and eradication should be possible if seedlings are removed over two growing seasons. Repeated burning of open sites is at best a temporary solution because the shrubs resprout.

James O. Luken, Department of Biological Sciences, Northern Kentucky University

Myoporum, a heavy seed producer, has spread in southern California's coastal areas. It gives rise to dense stands that expand each year, outcompeting other species, and if not controlled, can take over a landscape.

WHAT DOES IT LOOK LIKE?

Myoporum is a small evergreen tree or large shrub ranging from nine to 30 feet tall and 20 feet wide. It flourishes in coastal areas of southern California in heavy, alkaline, brackish and sandy soils. Its narrow 3- to 4-inch leaves are bright green and shiny, with translucent dots, and are toxic. Clusters of 2- to 6½-inch wide, bell-shaped white flowers with purple spots give way to pale to dark reddish purple fruits, which are less toxic than the leaves. Alone, it becomes a rather handsome multi-trunked, dome-shaped tree or shrub. With its dense foliage, rapid growth and habit of branching and spreading, it makes a thick and high hedge.

WHERE DID IT COME FROM? WHERE HAS IT SPREAD?

Native to New Zealand, myoporum has spread in coastal areas of southern California, forming dense single-species stands.

WHAT PROBLEMS DOES IT CAUSE?

Heavy seed production results in dense stands that enlarge each year and outcompete other species, which may also be affected by myoporum's toxic roots. If not controlled, the plants take over the landscape. Birds also spread the seeds, rapidly enlarging the affected area. Because dead branches accumulate inside large plants, myoporum burns fiercely, endangering homes in areas prone to wildfires. The leaves and fruits may be fatal to livestock.

HOW CAN IT BE CONTROLLED?

Pull the seedlings before they grow to more than 4 inches high or cut the trunk at ground level and apply 100 percent solution of glyphosate herbicide. Any trunk remaining above ground may resprout. If myoporum grows near natural areas, constant diligence must be exercised to keep the seedlings from overrunning the landscape.

Jo Kitz, Mountains Restoration Trust, Canoga Park, California

WHAT DOES IT LOOK LIKE?
Heavenly bamboo is a shrub that grows to 8 feet tall and is best known for its glossy, evergreen foliage and bright red berries in the fall and winter. Narrow, 2-inch long leaflets take on a burgundy color in winter, especially in the sun. Flowers are white.

WHERE DID IT COME FROM? WHERE HAS IT SPREAD?
Heavenly bamboo is native to India and eastern Asia. Cultivated as an ornamental since the mid-1950s, *N. domestica* and its various cultivars are common in southern gardens. Unfortunately, the berries are readily eaten by birds and as a result populations have escaped cultivation in the South, primarily northern Florida, southern Georgia and Alabama.

WHAT PROBLEMS DOES IT CAUSE?
The small shrubs are beginning to grow in the wild, primarily in pine flatwood communities in the Southeast. Typical of invasive non-native species, they are outcompeting native shrubs and associated understory herbaceous vegetation, decreasing native plant diversity and ultimately having a negative impact on associated wildlife.

HOW CAN IT BE CONTROLLED?
Hand-pulling seedlings is an effective method for decreasing populations. Unfortunately, the shrub develops a substantial taproot and therefore dig-

SHRUBS

Heavenly bamboo has escaped cultivation in the Southeast, and grows in the wild in pine flatwood communities. Like most invasive non-natives, it outcompetes native shrubs and their associated herbaceous vegetation, decreasing native plant diversity.

ging out larger specimens, while not impossible, tends to be difficult. Cutting the stems close to the ground and applying glyphosate or triclopyr herbicides seems to provide the best control.

Greg Jubinsky, Florida Department of Environmental Protection, Tallahassee

Common buckthorn has escaped cultivation throughout the northeastern and north central third of the U.S. It grows in woodlands, savannahs, prairies and abandoned fields, forming dense, impenetrable thickets.

SHRUBS

WHAT DOES IT LOOK LIKE?

Buckthorn is a shrub or small tree 6 to 9 feet tall, occasionally reaching 25 feet. It is named for the sharp thorns found at the tips of most branches. The bark is gray to blackish brown and rough when mature. Leaves are oblong to elliptical and toothed; the tips are rounded or pointed. First-year seedlings have two heart-shaped leaves. Buckthorn is one of the first shrubs to leaf out in the spring and one of the last to lose its leaves in the fall. Purple-black fruits are abundant on female trees from late summer to early spring.

WHERE DID IT COME FROM? WHERE HAS IT SPREAD?

Native to Eurasia, buckthorn was popular as a shelter-belt planting during the 1800s and now grows in the wild throughout the northeastern and north central third of the U.S. It prefers, but is not limited to, limy soils.

WHAT PROBLEMS DOES IT CAUSE?

Buckthorn can form dense, impenetrable thickets that displace native species. It is found in a variety of habitats, including woodlands, savannahs, prairies, abandoned agricultural fields and roadsides. All parts of the tree contain anthraquinones, which cause vomiting and diarrhea if eaten. It is also an alternate host for the fungus that causes oat rust.

HOW CAN IT BE CONTROLLED?

Buckthorn seedlings are easily pulled. Adults should be cut or girdled at the base. Resprouts that grow from the base should be cut, or the freshly cut trunk can be painted with a glyphosate herbicide to prevent resprouts. Since buckthorn enters winter dormancy later than most native species, the best time to treat it is mid to late autumn when non-target plants are least likely to be damaged.

Amy Samuels, Department of Environmental Forestry and Biology, State University of New York, College of Environmental Science and Forestry, Syracuse

WHAT DOES IT LOOK LIKE?

Smooth buckthorn is a multiple-stemmed shrub or small tree that grows 20 feet tall. The ½- to 3-inch long leaves lack teeth or lobes, and are shiny on top and moderately hairy underneath. Small, greenish flowers are borne on the current season's growth. The fruit initially is red but becomes black. Young plants less than 3 feet tall can fruit. The inner wood has a distinctive sulfur-like, light yellow color.

SHRUBS

Smooth buckthorn aggressively invades bogs, marshes, river banks, fens and pond margins, as well as dry sites such as sand forests, roadsides and prairies.

WHERE DID IT COME FROM? WHERE HAS IT SPREAD?

A native of Eurasia, this plant was introduced into the U.S. as an ornamental shrub in the 1800s. It has aggressively invaded wetlands, including bogs, marshes, river banks, fens and pond margins, but also has become established on dry sites such as sand forests, roadsides and prairies.

WHAT PROBLEMS DOES IT CAUSE?

Due to its prolific seed production and the dispersal of fruits by birds, smooth buckthorn rapidly invades wetland communities, crowding out native woody and herbaceous plants.

HOW CAN IT BE CONTROLLED?

Because smooth buckthorn is often intermingled with desirable native plants, control can be difficult. Once cut or wounded, it resprouts vigorously. Fire kills seedlings but only top-kills larger plants and usually needs to be followed up with a 50 percent solution of glyphosate herbicide to control sprouts. Where burning is inadvisable, foliar applications of 2 percent glyphosate during rapid spring growth are effective, provided that desirable plants are not damaged. Apply glyphosate to smaller stems immediately after cutting, using a squirt bottle or sponge applicator. Cut shrubs down to the base and then immediately apply 50 percent glyphosate around the periphery of the trunk for good, year-round control. Follow-up treatments may be necessary for the next several years.

Bill McClain, Illinois Department of Natural Resources

SHRUBS

Multiflora rose is recognized as a problem invader from Maine to Minnesota and south to Alabama, and has been classified as a noxious weed in several states.

cultivation and is recognized as a problem invader from Maine to Minnesota and south to Alabama. It has been classified as a noxious weed in several states, including New Jersey and Iowa.

WHAT PROBLEMS DOES IT CAUSE?

Multiflora rose is particularly damaging to pasture lands, where it has overtaken thousands of acres and displaced more palatable species. It has also usurped vast areas of native plant habitat. Roadsides, post-agricultural fields and other open habitats are very vulnerable to invasion, as are some wetlands. Birds are the primary means by which the shrub moves from place to place.

HOW CAN IT BE CONTROLLED?

Regular mowing inhibits seedling establishment in grassy areas. Medium to large shrubs can be removed with a weed-pulling tool or dug out by hand after the thorny tops have been cut away. If digging is not practical, cut and treat the stump with a glyphosate herbicide to prevent resprouting.

Glenn D. Dreyer, Connecticut College Arboretum, New London

WHAT DOES IT LOOK LIKE?

Multiflora rose is a large, vigorous shrub reaching 10 feet tall with long, arching stems. Clusters of single, one-inch wide, white flowers appear all over the plant in June, followed by clusters of quarter-inch red "hips" in August. The leaves are composed of five to ten 1-inch long, oval leaflets, and the branches are covered with stout thorns. Multiflora rose often forms dense, impenetrable thickets.

WHERE DID IT COME FROM? WHERE HAS IT SPREAD?

Introduced from Japan and Korea in the 1860s, it was originally planted as an ornamental shrub. In the 1930s, conservation agencies began to promote multiflora rose as a wildlife food and cover plant. It spread rapidly from

Beach naupaka is very popular with landscapers as a salt-tolerant shrub for coastal plantings, especially in southern Florida, where it colonizes sandy dunes and competes with native coastal vegetation.

SHRUBS

WHAT DOES IT LOOK LIKE?

Beach naupaka is a multi-stemmed shrub that forms rounded mounds from 3 to 6 and sometimes 10 feet tall. The succulent, light green leaves are somewhat spoon-shaped and clustered near the branch tips. Clustered flowers are white, sometimes blushed with pinkish purple. The round, ½-inch, pithy fruits are white. Two varieties are cultivated: *S. sericea* var. *sericea* has hairy leaves; *S. sericea* var. *taccada* has smooth leaves.

WHERE DID IT COME FROM?
WHERE HAS IT SPREAD?

Beach naupaka is native to the islands and coastal areas of the Indian and Pacific Oceans. It is very popular with landscapers as a salt-tolerant shrub for coastal plantings, especially in southern Florida. The fruits float and are carried by ocean currents to invade shorelines far away.

WHAT PROBLEMS DOES IT CAUSE?

Beach naupaka colonizes sandy dunes and competes with native coastal vegetation. It can quickly form extensive colonies, providing a seed source for more rapid dispersal to other shorelines. In southern Florida it competes directly with the related native inkberry, *Scaevola plumieri* (a state threatened species), which has stiff, dark green, glossy leaves and black fruit.

HOW CAN IT BE CONTROLLED?

Young specimens are easily hand-pulled and should be removed from the site because the plant roots easily from cuttings. Older plants should be mechanically removed by digging or hand-pulling and taken away, along with the seeds, from the site. If mechanical removal is not possible, cut the plants down to the ground and treat the stump with 50 percent triclopyr herbicide (amine formula) mixed with 50 percent water.

Roger L. Hammer, Metropolitan Dade County Park and Recreation Department

Brazilian pepper has invaded hundreds of thousands of acres of wetlands, hammocks, pinelands and other habitats throughout southern and central Florida, where it out-competes natives.

SHRUBS

WHAT DOES IT LOOK LIKE?

Brazilian pepper is a tree or multi-trunked shrub averaging 10 to 15 feet tall. Feather-like leaves have a red stem and midrib. Female trees have showy clusters of small, bright red fruit during winter. Leaves emit a turpentine-like odor when crushed.

WHERE DID IT COME FROM?
WHERE HAS IT SPREAD?

Native to Brazil, the plant tolerates moist to well-drained soils, and is an aggressive pioneer in disturbed sites such as roadsides, canal banks and abandoned farmland. Since its introduction into Florida in 1898 as an ornamental landscape tree, it has invaded hundreds of thousands of acres of wetlands, hammocks, pinelands and other areas throughout southern and central Florida. Seeds are spread principally by birds but are also eaten by mammals, especially raccoons.

WHAT PROBLEMS DOES IT CAUSE?

Brazilian pepper aggressively outcompetes native plant species in southern and central Florida, especially in pinelands, where it can overtake the understory and outcompete natives for light and nutrients. The plant is related to poison ivy and can cause skin irritation. The aromatic fruits are sold as "pink peppercorns" at gourmet shops, but may cause vomiting if eaten in quantity. There are reports that it has also begun to escape cultivation in southern California.

HOW CAN IT BE CONTROLLED?

Seedlings and saplings can be hand-pulled where soil disturbance is not an issue. Regrowth is rapid from seed, so follow-up control measures are usually necessary. Fire can be used in fire-adapted plant communities. A basal application of a triclopyr herbicide mixed with an oil diluent is effective. Targeting fruiting female trees will help eliminate future seed sources. Numerous follow-up treatments are always required to avoid reinfestation.

Roger L. Hammer, Metropolitan Dade County Park and Recreation Department

WHAT DOES IT LOOK LIKE?

An attractive multi-stemmed shrub growing 3 to 6 feet tall, Japanese spiraea is best recognized by its bright pink, flat-topped inflorescences that bloom in June and July. The narrow, toothed leaves taper to a pointed tip. The branches are wiry.

WHERE DID IT COME FROM? WHERE HAS IT SPREAD?

Introduced from Asia, Japanese spiraea is commonly sold through mail-order catalogs as well as at local nurseries. It has escaped cultivation and now grows in cool but not dry habitats from New England to Indiana south along the Appalachians to Tennessee and Georgia. *Spiraea japonica* can spread rapidly as it expands from the source area, readily infesting streambanks and roadsides and spreading into forests, thickets and overgrown fields.

WHAT PROBLEMS DOES IT CAUSE?

Dense "colonies" of Japanese spiraea can dominate streamsides, mossy springheads, moist cliffs and rich woodland understories, displacing or reducing populations of many native plants. As with most non-native, invasive species, more research is needed to determine the extent of its potential ecological disruption.

HOW CAN IT BE CONTROLLED?

Due to its vigorous, spreading root system and abundant seed production,

SHRUBS

Japanese spiraea grows in cool habitats from New England to Indiana and south to Tennessee and Georgia. It readily infests streambanks and roadsides, spreading into forests, thickets and overgrown fields.

control is difficult to achieve by pulling or cutting alone. Hand-pulling established plants is physically challenging and frustrating, as remaining small root segments appear to give rise to new stems. Cutting must usually be repeated, with particular attention to detection and removal of low-growing flower heads often hidden by other vegetation. A strong formulation of a glyphosate herbicide can be applied to the leaves of the growing plant prior to flowering (if applied after flowering, fruits should be clipped and removed). A second application may be necessary to completely kill this vigorous plant.

D. Daniel Boone, Appalachian Environmental Lab, University of Maryland

SHRUBS

Japanese yew is appearing in woodlots and young forests throughout southern New England. Beyond this range it may be in the early stages of escape—but it's so widely planted that it has the potential to become a serious weed.

WHAT DOES IT LOOK LIKE?

Japanese yew is a shrub or small, wide-spreading tree with evergreen, flattened needles. It may reach 40 feet in height, although many cultivated varieties are shorter and invariably pruned into small geometric shapes. Unpruned seedlings usually develop as single-stemmed plants. Female plants produce fleshy, bright red "fruits" a third of an inch wide and long, with a single seed. On older plants the bark is dark red and peels in long strips.

WHERE DID IT COME FROM? WHERE HAS IT SPREAD?

Native to Japan, Korea and Manchuria, Japanese yew was first imported to this country in 1855. Very widely planted due to its hardiness, shade tolerance and ability to withstand severe pruning, it is one of the most common landscape shrubs in the Northeast. Wild seedlings are also quite shade tolerant, appearing locally in woodlots and young forests throughout southern New England. It is clear that deer, which prefer yew over almost any other food, are controlling its spread in many locations.

WHAT PROBLEMS DOES IT CAUSE?

The extent of naturalization beyond this region has not yet been documented, and it may still be in the early stages of escape—but Japanese yew is so widely planted that it has the potential to become a serious problem.

HOW CAN IT BE CONTROLLED?

Seedlings and small saplings may be hand-pulled, pulled out with a weed-pulling tool or dug out. Larger plants tend to have large and difficult-to-remove root systems. However, yews cut to ground level rarely resprout.

Glenn D. Dreyer, Connecticut College Arboretum, New London

WHAT DOES IT LOOK LIKE?

Guelder rose is a deciduous shrub that grows up to 12 feet tall, with coarsely toothed maple-like leaves, usually with 3 shallow lobes. Guelder rose and native highbush cranberry (*Viburnum opulus* var. *americanum*) are varieties of the same shrub species, and distinguishing between them can be difficult. Guelder rose usually can be identified by the large saucer-shaped glands on the leafstalk.

WHERE DID IT COME FROM? WHERE HAS IT SPREAD?

Native to Eurasia, cultivated varieties of *Viburnum opulus* were planted as ornamentals starting in the second half of the 17th century. Today, it is found in the wild from Newfoundland to southern British Columbia and south to Virginia, eastern Nebraska, western South Dakota, Wyoming, Idaho and Washington. Able to tolerate a wide range of moisture and pH conditions, the shrub colonizes a variety of habitats, including forests, floodplains, wetlands, stream banks, bogs, fields and roadsides.

WHAT PROBLEMS DOES IT CAUSE?

Guelder rose is a cause for concern when it grows in natural areas and uncommon natural habitats, including fens, Great Lakes sandplains and limestone glades, where it may displace native plants. In the Midwest guelder rose is starting to naturalize in wetlands, and is deemed a threat to forests,

SHRUBS

Guelder rose now grows in the wild across the continent, from southern Canada south to Virginia, Nebraska and Washington State.

as well as degraded woodlands near urban and suburban areas. Guelder rose's reported ability to interbreed with the native highbush cranberry could produce a truly invasive shrub.

HOW CAN IT BE CONTROLLED?

Hand-pull plants less than 3 feet tall, before the root system becomes established. Taller shrubs should be cut at ground level. Natural area managers recommend applying a 20 percent solution of glyphosate herbicide to the cut stump to avoid resprouting, and chipping the brush to prevent seed dispersal.

Norma Kline, Pennsylvania Department of Conservation and Natural Resources

ANNUALS & PERENNIALS

WHAT DOES IT LOOK LIKE?

A succulent perennial with creeping branches that generally grows several feet in diameter and can reach 50 feet in diameter but more than 2 feet high. The leaves are three-sided, about the same length and girth as a pinky finger, and have slightly serrated outer edges that occur in pairs along branches. Large, 1- to 2-inch wide, pale yellow

Iceplant has invaded beach, dune, coastal scrub and coastal bluff communities throughout coastal California. It is especially common in heavily disturbed areas, along highways and on former military bases, where it can form nearly impenetrable mats that crowd out natives.

or pink flowers, each with many narrow petals, are produced from January through August. *C. edulis* is believed to readily hybridize with the smaller but generally similar *C. chilensis*, or "sea fig." Hybrids share traits of both parents and are likely to pose the same problems as *C. edulis*.

WHERE DID IT COME FROM? WHERE HAS IT SPREAD?

Native to coastal South Africa, highway iceplant was introduced into California for erosion control nearly 100 years ago. Spreading both vegetatively and by seed-dispersing mammals, it is now found in beach, dune, coastal scrub and coastal bluff communities throughout coastal California. It is especially common in heavily disturbed areas, along highways and on former military bases.

WHAT PROBLEMS DOES IT CAUSE?

Highway iceplant can form nearly impenetrable mats that crowd out native plants, and in many areas it has formed a virtual monoculture. It is able to grow in moist or very dry conditions. *C. edulis* is on the California Exotic Pest Plant Council's list of most invasive plants and poses a threat to several rare or endangered coastal species.

HOW CAN IT BE CONTROLLED?

Hand-pull individual plants. To prevent resprouting, remove any buried stems. Replant the area with natives and/or mulch to prevent re-establishment of iceplant seedlings. To remove large mats, pull and roll them from one side to the other like a carpet. Glyphosate herbicides have effectively controlled large patches as well.

Marc Albert, Golden Gate National Recreation Area, California

WHAT DOES IT LOOK LIKE?

Cornflower is notable for its brilliant, long-lasting blue flowers in summer. This annual can grow to 2 feet tall on tough, wiry stems. Some individuals in a population may have pink or white flowers. The leaves are narrow and cottony, with edges that are smooth or have a few teeth.

WHERE DID IT COME FROM? WHERE HAS IT SPREAD?

Originally from Europe and the Near East, cornflower is now found virtually worldwide. It has escaped from cultivation throughout the U.S.—to the point that many people are surprised to learn that it is not native. It is particularly invasive in native grasslands and prairies, especially in the Northwest, habitats that are becoming increasingly rare.

WHAT PROBLEMS DOES IT CAUSE?

Cornflower is a close relative of the knapweeds and starthistles, serious pests of agricultural and range lands as well as natural areas. Once established it produces ample seed with good viability, and populations increase quickly. Many grassland preserves are heavily infested with this attractive nuisance species.

HOW CAN IT BE CONTROLLED?

This is not a good ornamental to plant in gardens near grasslands that are not already infested. Yet cornflower (also commonly called bachelor's button) is a popular addition to commercial wildflower mixes, so read the labels of such products carefully!

Once established it is difficult to control. If the infestation is small, removing plants by hand before fruiting occurs should stop it (be sure to get most of the roots). If the population is large, removing flowers before

Cornflower, often assumed to be a native, has escaped cultivation throughout the U.S. and is particularly invasive in increasingly rare native grassland and prairie habitats, especially in the Northwest.

ANNUALS & PERENNIALS

seed set should eventually reduce the population size. Glyphosate herbicides will kill this species, but will also kill the surrounding native grasses and wildflowers.

Sarah Reichard, Department of Zoology, University of Washington, Seattle

WHAT DOES IT LOOK LIKE?

Crown vetch is a low-growing perennial used typically as a groundcover for roadside erosion control and mining reclamation. Pale pink, lavender or white pea-like blooms cover the plant from June to August. The foliage is dark green and fine textured. When dormant, crown vetch is recognizable by the large, brown, earth-hugging patches it forms. Because it grows

WHAT PROBLEMS DOES IT CAUSE?

Crown vetch climbs over shrubs and small trees, shading them out. It outcompetes native plants, degrades wildlife habitat and can form solid, single-species stands. Although it has the benefits noted above, its negatives outweigh them. Crown vetch is now being considered for control by federal, state and local agencies. It is already on Wisconsin's noxious weed list.

Crown vetch invades sunny areas in the Northeast and Midwest, climbing over shrubs and small trees, outcompeting natives and degrading wildlife habitat.

only 6 to 12 inches tall and therefore does not have to be mowed, it is considered a low-maintenance solution for steep slopes. Because it is a legume and fixes nitrogen in the soil, it is used on mining reclamation sites to rebuild the soil. Plants are also sold as groundcovers in mail-order garden catalogs.

WHERE DID IT COME FROM? WHERE HAS IT SPREAD?

Native to Europe, southwest Asia and northern Africa, crown vetch was introduced to the U.S. during the 1950s for erosion control. It invades sunny, upland areas in the Northeast and Midwest.

HOW CAN IT BE CONTROLLED?

The most important method of control is to *not* plant crown vetch in areas outside urban landscapes that have already been disturbed and where it cannot be contained, and should never be planted in a yard near the property line of a neighbor. Small areas can be controlled by applying a heavy mulch or shade cloth to deprive the plant of sunlight. Weed-b-Gon (2,4-D and dicamba) used with caution also provides effective control.

Bonnie Harper-Lore, Federal Highway Administration, Washington, D.C.

WHAT DOES IT LOOK LIKE?

This perennial of the sunflower family is crowned by a cluster of showy, bright purple composite flower heads 2 to 3 inches in diameter from April through July. One or several flower stalks rise from a bushy rosette up to 5 feet in diameter and 5 to 6 feet tall. The gray-green leaves are deeply lobed, and the bracts around flower heads sport stout, sharp spines.

WHERE DID IT COME FROM? WHERE HAS IT SPREAD?

This Mediterranean native is a cousin of the popular edible globe artichoke, and may, in fact, be a variety of the globe artichoke gone "wild." After escaping cultivation in the 1860s, it was reported to be well established in San Diego County by 1897. By 1933 it covered over 100,000 acres of ranch-land in four California counties. By the 1950s it occurred in some 31 counties and was declared an agricultural pest. From rangelands the plant spread into mixed native/non-native grasslands, non-grassy, herbaceous canyon bottoms, along stream banks and into openings in the chaparral and coastal sage scrub throughout the state.

WHAT PROBLEMS DOES IT CAUSE?

Dense single-species stands, up to 22,000 plants per acre, displace perennials, annuals and even grasses and make an impassable barrier for wildlife and cattle. They can displace endan-

ANNUALS & PERENNIALS

Wild artichoke invades grasslands, canyon bottoms, stream banks, chaparral and coastal sage scrub throughout California. Dense single-species stands displace natives.

gered native plants dependent on clay soils, to which they are well adapted.

HOW CAN IT BE CONTROLLED?

Hand-pull young seedlings. Hand dig larger, first-year plants. Glyphosate herbicides can control larger stands of adult plants that have deep tap roots. Applying herbicide to the cut "stump" is effective at any stage of growth, whereas foliar spraying is most effective when the plant is mature and bolting.

Mike Kelly, California Exotic Pest Plant Council, San Diego

ANNUALS &
PERENNIALS

Foxglove, a popular plant in perennial gardens, is common throughout
the U.S., especially in coastal areas
of the Pacific Northwest. It usually
colonizes disturbed lands such as
burned fields and logging clear-
cuts, and once established, seeds
itself vigorously.

WHAT DOES IT LOOK LIKE?

Foxglove sends up 3- to 4-foot spikes
of purple, white and pink flowers (all
colors may be on the same spike) from
May through July. The flowers are
large (to 2 inches long) and bell-
shaped. The plant is usually a biennial,
producing a basal rosette of fuzzy,
gray-green leaves the first year and
flowers the second year.

WHERE DID IT COME FROM? WHERE HAS IT SPREAD?

This species is so widely distributed it
is difficult to know exactly where it is
from, but it is believed to be native to
the western Mediterranean region. It
is common throughout the U.S., especially in coastal areas of the Pacific
Northwest. It usually colonizes disturbed areas such as burned fields and
logging cuts.

WHAT PROBLEMS DOES IT CAUSE?

Common foxglove is a popular plant in
perennial gardens, but once planted it
will seed itself throughout the garden
unless vigorously pursued. Wildlife
and cattle have died after grazing on
the plant, and almost every year people
die after drinking tea made of foxglove
leaves, the source of the heart stimu-
lant digitalis, when they thought they
had collected comfrey leaves.

HOW CAN IT BE CONTROLLED?

Foxglove can be controlled easily in
the first (vegetative) year by hand
removal. Repeated visits to the site to
remove new seedlings will be necessary. Glyphosate and other herbicides
appear to have only fair results.

*Sarah Reichard, Department of Zoology,
University of Washington, Seattle*

Fallopia japonica — Japanese knotweed

WHAT DOES IT LOOK LIKE?

Japanese knotweed looks like a shrub but has no woody tissue. Its stems, hollow and bamboo-like, can grow to over 13 feet tall. It sends up shoots in early spring from its large rhizomes. Its leaves are broad and taper to a fine point at the tip. Fleecy white flower clusters appear in late summer.

WHAT PROBLEMS DOES IT CAUSE?

Japanese knotweed is a particular problem along riverbanks and in other wet areas. It forms dense stands that exclude native vegetation and reduce wildlife habitat. It also causes flooding by decreasing water flow through river and stream channels.

Japanese knotweed (often known as *Polygonum cuspidatum*) is found throughout the eastern U.S., Colorado, Utah, northern California, Washington, Oregon and western Canada. Once established it is extremely difficult to eradicate.

ANNUALS & PERENNIALS

WHERE DID IT COME FROM? WHERE HAS IT SPREAD?

A native of eastern Asia, Japanese knotweed was introduced to North America as an ornamental in the late 19th century. Today it is found in virtually all states in the eastern U.S., and in Colorado, Utah, northern California, Washington, Oregon and Alaska, as well as lower Canada from Newfoundland to British Columbia. It spreads vegetatively—and rhizomes are dispersed in contaminated soil transported by humans and also washed downstream from established stands.

HOW CAN IT BE CONTROLLED?

Once Japanese knotweed is established it is extremely difficult to eradicate. Control small patches by digging out the entire plant, including even tiny pieces of rhizome, which can regrow. Control larger plants with persistent cutting throughout the growing season and/or repeated use of glyphosate herbicide. It will probably take more than one growing season to completely eradicate all but the smallest stands.

Leslie A. Seiger, Department of Biology, San Diego State University

WHAT DOES IT LOOK LIKE?

Baby's-breath is a much branched, dome-shaped and tumbleweed-like perennial in the carnation family that grows from 2 to 4 feet tall. The plant produces a profusion of tiny, ¼-inch, 5-petaled, white flowers, giving it an airy, delicate appearance. The leaves are small, gray-green and grow opposite each other, supported by wiry stems and a long, woody rhizome. Baby's-breath blooms in the summer.

WHAT PROBLEMS DOES IT CAUSE?

In Northern Michigan baby's-breath is invading the habitat occupied by *Cirsium pitcheri,* commonly known as pitcher's or dune thistle, a federal and state threatened species endemic to the Great Lakes. The open dune habitat on the perimeter of the Great Lakes, site of the largest system of freshwater dunes in the world, is vulnerable all along its shores to invasion by baby's-breath.

ANNUALS &
PERENNIALS

Baby's-breath has become a problem in Michigan's unique coastal zone, where it is colonizing the freshwater dunes along the Great Lakes, the largest such system in the world.

WHERE DID IT COME FROM? WHERE HAS IT SPREAD?

Baby's-breath is a native of Eastern Europe and Siberia, but was noted in the wild in the Chicago area by the 1930s. It colonizes disturbed areas, preferring full sun and slightly alkaline sands. In Michigan, baby's-breath is found on sandy roadsides, fields, shores, ditches and railroad embankments. More recently, it has spread to the freshwater dune systems along Lake Michigan.

HOW CAN IT BE CONTROLLED?

Control baby's-breath by cutting the root with a spade-type shovel on an angle below the caudex (the underground stem) and at least 4 inches below ground. Remove the aboveground portion but leave the root in place and monitor for resprouting, and retreat as necessary. Early in the growing season you can also spot-burn plants with a hand-held propane torch.

Kim D. Herman, Natural Heritage Program, Michigan Department of Natural Resources

WHAT DOES IT LOOK LIKE?

A short-lived perennial of the mustard family, dame's rocket reaches a height of 2 to 3 feet. At the top of the single stalk it bears loose clusters of ¾- to 1-inch, four-petaled flowers that are purple, white or lilac and fragrant, especially in the evening. It blooms in early summer of the year following seed germination. The leaves are toothed and lance-shaped, with pointed tips. The narrow fruits grow up to 5 inches long. It is often confused with phlox, which has five, not four, flower petals.

WHERE DID IT COME FROM? WHERE HAS IT SPREAD?

A native of Europe, dame's rocket was introduced as a garden plant during the Colonial period, probably on the East Coast. It easily escaped cultivation and spread across most of the continent. By the end of the 19th century, it was so well established in alluvial woods, along roadsides and edges of woods that it is often assumed to be a native wildflower.

WHAT PROBLEMS DOES IT CAUSE?

Although it is not a large-scale invasive, dame's rocket can dominate moist areas of meadow, forest edge and alluvial woods to the exclusion of native plants. It spreads rapidly from seed.

HOW CAN IT BE CONTROLLED?

Small numbers of plants can be hand-pulled. Larger infestations can be controlled by applying a glyphosate herbicide in early spring or late fall. Check the area for several years to eliminate

ANNUALS & PERENNIALS

Dame's rocket so easily escaped cultivation and spread across the continent that many people now believe it to be a native wildflower. It can dominate moist areas of meadow, forest edge and alluvial woods to the exclusion of native plants, spreading rapidly by seed.

new plants that germinate from the original seedbank. Dame's rocket should not be included in wildflower mixes for roadside plantings.

Steve Young, New York State Natural Heritage Program

WHAT DOES IT LOOK LIKE?
This leguminous perennial has a growth habit ranging from sprawling to erect, 12 to 24 inches tall. Leaves consist of three clover-like leaflets on a short stem, with two additional leaflets at the stem base. The pea- or clover-like flowers are bright yellow, sometimes tinged with red, about ½inch long and typically in clusters of three to 12 arising from a common point. One-inch long brown seed pods are produced in clusters that resemble a bird's foot, giving the plant its common name.

WHERE DID IT COME FROM? WHERE HAS IT SPREAD?
Native to Europe, bird's-foot trefoil was introduced into New York around 1880. Its 25 commercially available cultivars have been planted throughout the U.S. and Canada for livestock forage and erosion control along roadsides. It grows best in the Midwest and along the St. Lawrence River and is most problematic in tallgrass prairies.

WHAT PROBLEMS DOES IT CAUSE?
Trefoil can form thick mats, choking out most other vegetation. Prescribed burning increases seed germination and aids in the establishment of new seedlings, making it a troublesome species in native tallgrass prairie.

Bird's-foot trefoil has been planted throughout the U.S. and Canada for livestock forage and erosion control along roadsides. It thrives in the Midwest and along the St. Lawrence River and is most problematic in tallgrass prairies.

HOW CAN IT BE CONTROLLED?
Mowing more than once every 3 weeks at a height of less than 2 inches seems to control this plant effectively; this method may have to be used over the course of several years to eliminate the plants. Herbicides containing MCPA and clopyralid provide effective control when applied as a foliar spray.

Brian Winter and Gordon Yalch, The Nature Conservancy Minnesota Western Preserves Office

WHAT DOES IT LOOK LIKE?

Loosestrife is a perennial best known for its long, showy spikes of purple flowers, which dominate infested wetlands between June and September. The plant can grow 6 to 10 feet tall with 30 to 50 squared stems. Leaves are lance-shaped and grow opposite each other on the stem or in whorls of three.

WHERE DID IT COME FROM? WHERE HAS IT SPREAD?

A native of Eurasia, loosestrife was introduced to the northeastern U.S. in the early 1800s. It has since spread through the temperate parts of North America and is expanding its range. It is most abundant in the Northeast, colonizing wetland habitats, including meadows, marshes, river banks and shores of lakes and ponds.

WHAT PROBLEMS DOES IT CAUSE?

Extensive, permanent stands replace native vegetation, threaten rare and endangered plant species and reduce the availability of food and shelter for wildlife. Loosestrife has been declared a noxious weed in many states and provinces, where its sale and growth are prohibited. However, cultivars of *L. salicaria* and *L. virgatum* (which is probably the same species) are widely available.

HOW CAN IT BE CONTROLLED?

According to recent research, even so-called infertile cultivars produce viable seeds and should not be used. Individ-ual plants can be hand-pulled before seed set. Larger populations are extremely difficult to control—do not attempt to dig out roots because soil disturbance may enhance the spread. Frequent cutting of stems at ground level is effective but needs to be continued for several years (burn the cut stems because plants resprout from fragments). While natural area man-

Purple loosestrife is most abundant in the Northeast, colonizing wetland habitats—meadows, marshes, river banks and shores of lakes and ponds—and is expanding its range.

ANNUALS & PERENNIALS

agers successfully use spot treatments of glyphosate herbicide, constant monitoring is necessary due to the likelihood that plants will become reestablished.

Bernd Blossey, College of Agriculture and Life Sciences, Cornell University, Ithaca, New York

WHAT DOES IT LOOK LIKE?

Before flowering, sulfur cinquefoil looks like a hairy marijuana plant because of the shape of the leaves. These palmately compound leaves have 5 to 7 leaflets with toothed edges. Leaf size and leafstalk length decrease from the lower stem to the flowering top. There are usually one to several upright, 12- to 28-inch tall stems with no or only a few slender branches.

ANNUALS & PERENNIALS

Sulfur cinquefoil is a well established weed in the Northeast and the Great Lakes region, and is rapidly expanding into the western states and Canada.

Numerous flowers with pale sulfur-yellow petals are produced at the top of the stalks from May to July. Sulfur cinquefoil is often confused with native *Potentilla* species. Long right-angled hairs on the leaves and stems, many stem leaves but few basal leaves on mature plants, and a heavily wrinkled seed coat help distinguish it from native cinquefoils.

WHERE DID IT COME FROM? WHERE HAS IT SPREAD?

Native to the Mediterranean region, sulfur cinquefoil had become well established in the Northeast and the Great Lakes region by the 1950s. Expansion in the western U.S. and Canada is now proceeding exponentially.

WHAT PROBLEMS DOES IT CAUSE?

This long-lived perennial is very competitive in native grasslands and can even become dominant in forest habitats where tree cover has been reduced. Drought tolerance and relative unpalatability to grazing animals enhance its competitiveness. Sulfur cinquefoil is becoming one of the most serious wildland invaders in the northern Rockies.

HOW CAN IT BE CONTROLLED?

Sulfur cinquefoil is easily removed by slipping a sturdy digging tool under the crown and woody rootstock. Watch for seedlings, as seeds remain viable in the soil for at least three years. Picloram or 2,4-D herbicides provide the only known effective control for large infestations at this time.

Peter Rice, Division of Biological Sciences, University of Montana at Missoula

WHAT DOES IT LOOK LIKE?

Vinca is a trailing groundcover with glossy, evergreen leaves up to 2 inches long that taper at both ends and grow opposite each other on the stem. One-inch wide flowers are produced in very early spring and look like small blue, lilac or white stars. Vinca sometimes flowers throughout the summer and fall. Various cultivars exhibit a wider range of flower color and leaf variegation.

WHERE DID IT COME FROM? WHERE HAS IT SPREAD?

Native to Europe, periwinkle was valued as a medicinal herb and aphrodisiac. Its exact date of introduction is unknown, but it has a long history as a garden plant in the U.S. It has escaped cultivation in most of the northeastern and north central states. It persists in shady areas of second-growth woods, usually near the site of the original planting. Its close relative, *V. major,* is troublesome in sheltered canyon bottoms and floodplains in the Southwest and Canada and can be distinguished from *V. minor* by its larger, 2-inch blooms and leaves with rounded bases and tapered tips.

WHAT PROBLEMS DOES IT CAUSE?

Although periwinkle does not spread to new areas by seed, it persists in its original planting site, often for decades. A single clone can spread vegetatively and cover large areas of woodland understory, crowding out all native herbaceous vegetation.

HOW CAN IT BE CONTROLLED?

Both *Vinca minor* and *V. major* can be removed mechanically by raising the runners with a rake and mowing, or by digging up the plants. Be sure to remove all of the plant, as the stems root easily whenever the nodes touch the ground. These species can also be controlled by cutting the plants in early to late spring during active plant

ANNUALS & PERENNIALS

Vinca minor **is now found in most of the northeastern and north central states, persisting in shady areas of second-growth woods and spreading from its original planting.**

growth, followed by an application of a glyphosate herbicide. Any remaining plants can be removed by hand or spot-treated with the herbicide.

Steve Young, New York State Natural Heritage Program

WHAT DOES IT LOOK LIKE?

Giant reed is one of the largest grasses in the world, reaching more than 30 feet tall. It forms dense bunches from branching, tuberous rhizomes. In late summer mature plants produce dense, whitish, terminal flower clusters. The

GRASSES

Giant reed invades freshwater habitats in warmer climates from California to Maryland. Once established, it can form huge clones covering hundreds of acres.

seeds apparently are sterile, and the plant reproduces vegetatively from fragments of stems and rhizomes.

WHERE DID IT COME FROM? WHERE HAS IT SPREAD?

A native of western Asia, northern Africa and southern Europe, giant reed was introduced from the Mediterranean in the early 1800s. It has been used for erosion control, as an ornamental, as a wind-break, to thatch roofs and to make clarinet and bassoon reeds. It invades freshwater habitats in warmer climates from California to Maryland.

WHAT PROBLEMS DOES IT CAUSE?

Once established, giant reed can form huge clones, sometimes covering hundreds of acres. It provides neither food nor habitat for native wildlife. It is highly flammable and resprouts quickly after burning. Fires help transform communities of native plants into solid stands of giant reed, changing riverbank forests from flood- to fire-defined habitats. The plant is considered one of the primary threats to native riparian habitats in the Southwest, and especially in California.

HOW CAN IT BE CONTROLLED?

Herbicides must be used to ensure that the root mass is killed because even tiny fragments of rhizome can grow into new colonies. Both glyphosate and fluazipop herbicides have proven effective, especially when applied after flowering. Because this species tends to spread downstream, it's important to remove infestations from the upper reaches of a watershed first.

Gary Bell, The Nature Conservancy, Temecula, California

WHAT DO THEY LOOK LIKE?

Both are perennial grasses with long leaves rising from a tufted base. The two species are very similar to each other but jubata grass has longer flowering stems and darker, more brownish or purplish plumes, and its flowering stems are twice as high as its foliage. At the terminal ends of the stems are purplish to tawny white, softly hairy plumes. Flowering typically occurs in late summer but occasionally in the spring as well. Jubata grass is also much more widespread than its relative.

Unlike those of jubata grass, the

WHERE DID THEY COME FROM? WHERE HAVE THEY SPREAD?

C. jubata is native to Argentina and along the Andes of Bolivia, Peru and Ecuador, where it can grow from sea level to 11,000 feet. It may have entered California from France through the horticultural trade in the early 1900s. Today it is widespread along the Pacific Coast from San Diego north to the Oregon border.

C. selloana is a native of Argentina, southern Brazil and Uruguay, where it grows in damp soil along river margins. It was introduced as an ornamental in California in 1848. Nurserymen from

Jubata grass is widespread along the Pacific Coast from San Diego north to the Oregon border. Each plume can contain over 100,000 seeds and seedlings can become established rapidly on bare soil or in coastal forests after cutting.

GRASSES

flowering stems of pampas grass are only slightly taller than the foliage. The flower plumes are light violet to silvery white. Plants produce either all male or all female flowers. Because male plants are rare in the U.S., flowers typically do not produce viable seed. Flowering generally occurs in late spring to early summer.

Santa Barbara selected for female plants because they produce more attractive, fluffier plumes. Although it has become a weedy problem in some coastal areas between San Francisco and San Diego, the plant is still grown as an ornamental throughout California.

continues on the next page

continued from the preceding page

C. jubata is also a problem along streams in the mountains of southern Arizona.

WHAT PROBLEMS DO THEY CAUSE?
Jubata grass reproduces in an unusual way—it is apomictic—that is, seeds are produced without pollen. Each plume can contain over 100,000 seeds, which can disperse long distances by wind. Seedlings can become established rapidly on bare, wet, sandy soil or in coastal forests following burning or clear cutting. When male pampas grass plants are present, viable seeds can be produced, and these, too, can be dispersed long distances by wind. The seeds germinate and grow rapidly in open sandy soils with adequate moisture.

Mature plants of both species can displace native species rapidly, threatening native coastal ecosystems, and in the case of jubata grass, forest re-establishment as well.

HOW CAN THEY BE CONTROLLED?
Because of the sensitivity of the sites occupied by jubata and pampas grass, few control strategies are available. Mechanically removing plants before flowering is effective, provided all above-ground portions of the stem are severed from the root. This is best done with heavy digging equipment or a heavy hoe. Both species of *Cortaderia* will be extremely difficult to hand-pull once they have grown beyond the seedling stage. Where mechanical control is not practical, spot treatment with a glyphosate herbicide provides good control. However, it's important to get good coverage and deep penetration.

Joseph M. Di Tomaso, Cooperative Extension, University of California at Davis

GRASSES

Pampas grass is an occasional problem in some of California's coastal areas and is still grown as an ornamental statewide.

WHAT DOES IT LOOK LIKE?

Tall fescue is a coarse, perennial, cool-season grass that grows in heavy clumps and can form solid stands. Older leaves are dark green, with a rough, waxy cuticle at the top. Leaves are encircled by the collar of the leaf sheath. The flower head (inflorescence) is 2 to 10 inches long, and may nod at the tip.

WHERE DID IT COME FROM? WHERE HAS IT SPREAD?

A native of Europe, tall fescue has been used for erosion control, as a pasture grass and, recently, a drought-resistant turfgrass. It is adapted to a variety of habitats, soils and climates, and ranges from Florida and Texas to Canada. It is invasive throughout the warmer, drier areas in this range, and also in some areas in California and the Northwest.

WHAT PROBLEMS DOES IT CAUSE?

Tall fescue has replaced diverse native herbaceous communities, especially in remnant prairies of the Midwest and northern Texas. Many varieties are infected with an endophytic fungus that may make this grass more drought tolerant, more effective at utilizing nitrogen and probably allelopathic (capable of chemically suppressing competing species). This allelochemical is thought to be poisonous not only to other plants, but also to cattle and other herbivores.

HOW CAN IT BE CONTROLLED?

Light infestations can be controlled by spot applications of a glyphosate herbicide prior to the emergence of the grass flowers and when other desirable species are dormant. In the Midwest, fall applications after the first hard freeze have been successful. Heavy infestations over large areas are probably best treated by prescribed fire, but only qualified people should undertake prescribed burning. Burn when the fescue is flowering, when the plant's energy reserves are low and regrowth will be more difficult. Repeat burning annually for several years.

James A. Eidson, The Nature Conservancy of Texas

GRASSES

Tall fescue invades remnant prairies in the Midwest, eastern Plains and north Texas.

WHAT DOES IT LOOK LIKE?

Cogongrass is a tall grass (average 3 feet) that spreads extensively, unlike clumping ornamental grasses. Erect leaves arising from the base are about three quarters of an inch wide and have a white, off-center midvein. Spike-like flower stalks are topped by silky white plumes. The ornamental cultivar 'Red Baron' (also called Japanese Bloodgrass or 'Rubra') has reddish leaves.

WHERE DID IT COME FROM? WHERE HAS IT SPREAD?

Cogongrass is native to southeast Asia and is now a widespread weed

Cogongrass is now widespread throughout subtropical and tropical regions, and is considered one of the world's worst weeds.

throughout subtropical and tropical regions. It was introduced into Alabama and Mississippi in the early 1900s for forage and soil stabilization and has spread by underground stems and seed throughout the Gulf Coast states. Ornamental cultivars have apparently not yet spread beyond gardens.

WHAT PROBLEMS DOES IT CAUSE?

Cogongrass, considered one of the world's worst weeds, is on the Federal Noxious Weed List. It infests road-sides, surface-mined lands and pine plantations, and is inferior livestock forage in pastures. Cogongrass invades a wide variety of natural habitats such as desert dunes, wetlands, savannahs and forests, where it out-competes wild plants, is poor wildlife habitat and is highly flammable.

The ornamental 'Red Baron' is freeze-tolerant, and there is some concern that hybridization with this cultivar might enhance the cold hardiness of cogongrass, so cultivation of 'Red Baron' is not recommended.

HOW CAN IT BE CONTROLLED?

In gardens dig and remove all underground stems. In agricultural areas cogongrass is controlled by discing followed by one or more applications of glyphosate or imazapyr herbicide. In natural areas where discing is not advisable, one or more applications of glyphosate in the fall is recommended. Burning several months before treating enhances uptake of the herbicide.

Carol Lippincott and Sandra McDonald, University of Florida, Gainesville

GRASSES

WHAT DOES IT LOOK LIKE?

This hardy perennial grass grows in dense, bushy, upright and arching clumps 6 to 10 feet tall. The leaf blades, with a distinct whitish midrib, are 3½ feet long and less than an inch wide, with sharp, recurving, slender tips. The silky, plume-like terminal panicle is 6 to 24 inches long, silvery to pale pink and showiest in autumn.

WHERE DID IT COME FROM? WHERE HAS IT SPREAD?

Chinese silver grass, native to eastern Asia, has become a popular ornamental grass in recent years. It has spread to disturbed sites along roadsides, woodland borders and clearings within wooded areas. It is found in pockets throughout the eastern U.S. from Florida to Texas, north to Massachusetts and New York.

WHAT PROBLEMS DOES IT CAUSE?

Once Chinese silver grass escapes, it tends to remain in the new site or slowly spread into highly disturbed areas, such as along roadsides. Because it currently appears to be only slightly invasive, several eastern states have placed this species on their "watch" lists. More information is needed on the movement and invasive potential of this ornamental grass.

HOW CAN IT BE CONTROLLED?

Spot-treat with a glyphosate herbicide in spring when the new shoots are 4 to 6 inches tall. This treatment may be continued periodically until flowering. Since Chinese silver grass spreads by rhizomes, be sure to spot-treat new shoots arising from the base of the plant.

Patricia Dalton Haragan, Davies Herbarium, University of Louisville, Kentucky

GRASSES

Chinese silver grass grows in clearings in wooded areas throughout the eastern U.S. from Florida to Texas, north to Massachusetts and New York. As yet, the grass is not very invasive, but it's begun to show up on experts' "to watch" lists.

WHAT DOES IT LOOK LIKE?

Perennial reed canary grass has stems 3 to 7 feet high and flat leaf blades ¼- to ¾-inch wide. Varieties used horticulturally are best known for their variegated light green- and white-striped leaves. Plants flower in mid-June, followed shortly thereafter by production of oily-feeling seeds.

WHERE DID IT COME FROM? WHERE HAS IT SPREAD?

Reed canary grass, which was intro-

clumps that coalesce into single-species stands often covering large acreages at the expense of native wetland species, which quickly decline under its cover.

HOW CAN IT BE CONTROLLED?

Reed canary grass grows in dense mats that can be difficult to manage. In the garden, cultivars can be hand-pulled. In the wild, mowing, prescribed burning and wick application (see page 22) of a glyphosate herbicide licensed for use

GRASSES

Reed canary grass (lower right) grows freely across the continent. It invades wetland habitats such as wet prairies in the Midwest, and is also rapidly invading alpine and montane habitats in the western U.S. and Canada.

duced for its forage value in the northern U.S. from Europe and Asia, is found widely from coast to coast today. It occupies drainage ways, has invaded many wetland habitats, including wet prairies in the Midwest, and is rapidly invading alpine and montane habitats in western states and Canada.

WHAT PROBLEMS DOES IT CAUSE?

In the wild, reed canary grass, which spreads vegetatively, forms dense

over water have been most effective—and in wetland environments where burning is not effective, herbicides are the only option. Best control often is achieved with several rounds of burning and use of herbicide on green resprouts. Planting native wetland grasses and sedges helps prevent re-invasion of reed canary grass.

Steven L. Apfelbaum, Applied Ecological Services, Inc., Brodhead, Wisconsin

WHAT DOES IT LOOK LIKE?

This perennial vine is most remarkable in autumn when its abundant clusters of large, shiny berries turn blue and purple mottled with white and gray. It is frequently mistaken for a grape because of its similar leaf shape, which varies from deeply lobed to "entire," with a continuous unbroken edge. The leaves are sometimes variegated. Tiny yellow blooms appear in mid-summer.

WHERE DID IT COME FROM? WHERE HAS IT SPREAD?

Introduced from northeast Asia in 1870, porcelain berry initially was planted on estates in the East. Today, it is very abundant in the Northeast coastal zone between Boston and Washington, D.C. It colonizes open, sunny habitats subject to repeated disturbance, such as highway shoulders, railroad tracks, river banks, shorelines, fields, forest edges and gaps in woodlands.

WHAT PROBLEMS DOES IT CAUSE?

Porcelain berry forms extensive tangles that blanket the ground and trees and shrubs of woodland edges, greatly reducing the diversity of species. Festooned trees are more vulnerable to wind damage. The seeds have a very high germination rate, and the plant also is able to reproduce vegetatively from stem or root segments.

HOW CAN IT BE CONTROLLED?

Once established, porcelain berry is extremely difficult to control. The extensive root system cannot be dug out. The above-ground vines can be cut by hand and pulled from trees. Repeated cutting or mowing will contain the vine but not eradicate it. The best method of control is to gradually shade it out by planting trees or allowing existing trees to mature, while keeping them free of vines. Chemical control produces mixed results; foliar application of a glyphosate herbicide in early autumn is most effective.

Susan Antenen, The Nature Conservancy, Long Island Chapter

Porcelain berry grows abundantly along the Northeast coast from Boston to Washington, D.C. It overtakes open, sunny, disturbed habitats such as river banks, railroad tracks and forest edges.

VINES

WHAT DOES IT LOOK LIKE?

A deciduous, twining, woody vine with abundant bright yellow and red fruits and yellow fall leaf color. Vines can grow to over five inches in diameter and 60 feet long. The spring-blooming flowers are inconspicuous. The leaves, oval to nearly round, occur singly at different heights and on different sides of the stem. The only reliable way to differentiate this vine from the native American bittersweet (*Celastrus scandens*) is to look at the fruits, which in Oriental bittersweet appear all along the stems in clusters of three to seven; American bittersweet produces larger clusters of fruit only at the tips of stems.

WHERE DID IT COME FROM? WHERE HAS IT SPREAD?

Native to Japan, Korea and China, Oriental bittersweet was brought to North America in the mid 1800s. By 1974 it had escaped cultivation in 21 states, from Maine to Georgia and west at least to Minnesota. Preferred habitats are open woods, thickets and road-sides. Birds and people who use the fruit in dried arrangements are its primary means of dispersal.

WHAT PROBLEMS DOES IT CAUSE?

The vine climbs up surrounding plants, shading their leaves . It also aggressively competes for space, water and nutrients. Its twining action constricts the host plant's stem, impeding sap flow. Dense infestations make the host plant top-heavy and prone to wind damage. Oriental bittersweet also root suckers vigorously, especially when the top is damaged. It is a menace to natural and landscaped areas throughout the East. Upland meadows, thickets and young forests are most vulnerable.

HOW CAN IT BE CONTROLLED?

Regular mowing will exclude bittersweet. Triclopyr herbicides have proved effective both as foliar sprays and applied on cut stumps.

Glenn D. Dreyer, Connecticut College Arboretum, New London

VINES

Oriental bittersweet has escaped cultivation in 21 states, from Maine to Georgia and west as far as Minnesota. It invades open woods, thickets and roadsides, where it climbs atop natives.

WHAT DOES IT LOOK LIKE?

A woody vine with dark green leaves. Juvenile leaves have lighter-colored veins and three to five lobes. Mature leaves, which form when the plant reaches reproductive age (usually 10 years) are egg-shaped in outline. In autumn flowers are produced in clusters at the tips of stems and are very attractive to bees. Non-native birds such as starlings eat the dark blue or purplish fruits.

WHERE DID IT COME FROM? WHERE HAS IT SPREAD?

Native to Eurasia, English ivy was introduced into North America in early colonial times. The species, which can tolerate lots of shade, is found in upland forests, especially those relatively close to urban areas where it is grown. It is found in Middle Atlantic, Southeast and West Coast states. The California Exotic Pest Plant Council considers it a serious problem. It is especially invasive in western Oregon and Washington where citizens groups spend their Saturdays trying to remove it from forests.

WHAT PROBLEMS DOES IT CAUSE?

The plant forms "ivy deserts" in forests, inhibiting the regeneration of wildflowers, trees and shrubs. It is not used by native wildlife. It tends to grow up tree trunks, adding weight that may increase storm damage.

HOW CAN IT BE CONTROLLED?

The best control is probably hand removal, using pruners to cut the vines and then pulling the plants from the forest floor and trees. Be careful to minimize soil disturbance, which enhances conditions for ivy and other aggressive species. Planting native species will help prevent undesirable plants from becoming established. One extreme method used with some success is burning the plants repeatedly with a blow torch; the energy the plant needs to regrow eventually is depleted. English ivy's waxy leaves are almost impervious to herbicides.

Sarah Reichard, Department of Zoology, University of Washington, Seattle

VINES

English ivy is especially invasive in western Oregon and Washington and it is also considered a serious problem by the California Exotic Pest Plant Council.

WHAT DO THEY LOOK LIKE?

Both of these jasmines are woody vines. *J. fluminense*, commonly known as Brazilian jasmine, has compound leaves composed of three leathery leaflets growing opposite each other on the stem. *J. dichotomum*, or Gold Coast jasmine, has glossy, leathery leaves that grow opposite each other on the stem. Unlike those of Brazilian jasmine, the leaves of this species are not compound, or divided into leaflets. Both species of jasmine produce very fragrant, multi-petalled, white flowers throughout the year but peaking in spring and early summer. The fruits of both species are small, round, fleshy and black, and ripe fruit can be found from summer into early winter.

WHERE DID THEY COME FROM? WHERE HAVE THEY SPREAD?

Gold Coast jasmine is a native of tropical Africa. Although Brazilian jasmine is also native to Africa, it was first described from Brazil, where it was introduced by Portuguese explorers. The renowned plant explorer Dr. David Fairchild introduced these and many other plants into cultivation in the United States—Brazilian jasmine in Florida in 1923, and Gold Coast jasmine in 1927. The enchanting nighttime fragrance of both species has made them popular landscape plants. However, both Gold Coast jasmine and Brazilian jasmine have escaped cultivation and are vigorously invading undisturbed hardwood forests as well as cultivated grounds and disturbed sites throughout Florida south of Gainesville.

WHAT PROBLEMS DO THEY CAUSE?

Gold Coast and Brazilian jasmine are both capable of completely enshrouding native vegetation. They can climb high into the canopy of mature forests, cutting off natural light and reducing the diversity of native species. Seeds are

VINES

Brazilian (left) and Gold Coast jasmine can both completely enshroud native vegetation and climb high into the canopy of mature forests, cutting off natural light and reducing the diversity of native species.

spread from landscape plants into forests by birds, and once established in natural forest communities, the seeds are further dispersed by raccoons. Other species of jasmine have also escaped cultivation in Florida, notably star jasmine, *J. multiflorum,* yellow jasmine, *J. mesnyi,* poet's jasmine, *J. officinale* and shining jasmine, *J. nitidum.* At present, however, Gold Coast and Brazilian jasmine are wreaking the greatest environmental havoc because of their aggressive nature and their ability to invade intact, undisturbed hardwood forests.

HOW CAN THEY BE CONTROLLED?
Dense concentrations of jasmine seedlings can be found sprouting from raccoon droppings. These and other seedlings can be hand-pulled. The best control of large, mature, woody vines is to cut them off at ground level and treat the cut stumps with a triclopyr herbicide mixed with 50 percent water. Pulling vines off of trees and shrubs in natural forest communities is not recommended because it causes considerable damage to the supporting native vegetation. Numerous follow-up inspections and treatments will be necessary in subsequent years to control the seedlings of these aggressive vines.

Roger L. Hammer, Metropolitan Dade County Park and Recreation Department

VINES

Like Brazilian jasmine, Gold Coast jasmine is a vigorous invader of hardwood forests and cultivated grounds throughout Florida, yet is still planted for its fragrance.

WHAT DOES IT LOOK LIKE?

Japanese honeysuckle is a woody vine with very fragrant white tubular flowers that grow in pairs and turn yellow as they age. The vine is evergreen in the South and semi-evergreen in the North. It is easily distinguished from native honeysuckle vines by its upper leaves, which are distinctly separate, and by its black to purple berries; the leaves of native honeysuckle vines are joined together around the stem, and the berries are red to orange.

WHERE DID IT COME FROM? WHERE HAS IT SPREAD?

Native to east Asia, Japanese honeysuckle was introduced into New York in 1806 as a landscape plant. It has spread throughout the eastern half of the U.S. from Massachusetts west to central Illinois and Missouri and south to Kansas, Texas and Florida and is problematic throughout this range. The vine, which is spread by birds that eat the fruits, is common in fields, forest openings and edges, along fencerows and on roadsides. In Illinois, its sale and distribution are prohibited.

VINES

Japanese honeysuckle is invasive from Massachusetts to central Illinois and Missouri and south to Kansas, Texas and Florida. The plant travels as birds eat and drop its fruits.

WHAT PROBLEMS DOES IT CAUSE?

Japanese honeysuckle spreads rapidly, overtopping and literally smothering surrounding small trees and shrubs. It may form a scattered ground layer on the shady floor of forests but will grow quickly into the canopy if a treefall or other disturbance increases light levels.

HOW CAN IT BE CONTROLLED?

Watch for and immediately destroy small plants, which are difficult to locate until well established and growing over other vegetation. Once plants are established the most effective control is foliar application of 1.5 percent glyphosate herbicide shortly after the first killing frost, when native plants are dormant. The temperature should be near or preferably above freezing, and applications within two days of the first killing frost and before the first hard frost are most effective. Check treated plants at the end of the second growing season, as they can resprout. Pulling, cutting, mowing or burning generally stimulate dense re-growth.

Victoria Nuzzo, Native Landscapes, Rockford, Illinois

WHAT DOES IT LOOK LIKE?

The mid-rib, or rachis, of this lacy, bright green, vining fern twines around small stems and branches of trees. The rachis is wiry, with widely spaced, short stems that support the pinnae (groups of leaflets), which are subdivided into two or three roughly triangular leaflets up to 3 inches long and 1 inch wide.

WHERE DID IT COME FROM? WHERE HAS IT SPREAD?

Native to eastern Asia and tropical Australia, Japanese climbing fern is a problem weed from central Florida west across the southern half of the Gulf states, invading pinelands in Florida, cypress swamps in Louisiana and beech forests in east Texas. Related non-native *Lygodium microphyllum,* with once-divided pinnae, has invaded cypress swamps and pinelands in Jonathan Dickinson State Park near West Palm Beach, Florida. Large infestations are also further south along the Loxahatchee River and Loxahatchee Slough.

WHAT PROBLEMS DOES IT CAUSE?

Japanese climbing fern can quickly climb to the canopy where it forms dense mats that shade out the trees and shrubs it covers, weakening or killing them. It can carry fires from ground level to the forest canopy; native plants in many of the forest and swamp habitats Japanese climbing fern invades are adapted to ground fires but are killed or severely damaged by crown fires.

HOW CAN IT BE CONTROLLED?

Control small infestations with repeated pulling and/or cutting. Larger infestations are more problematic. Managers at Florida Caverns State Park on the Florida panhandle pull the vines down from the trees and spray the foliage with a mixture of 15 percent triclopyr and 85 percent oil surfactant, with no water added.

John M. Randall, The Nature Conservancy, Davis, California

VINES

Japanese climbing fern has invaded Florida's pinelands, cypress swamps in Louisiana and beech forests in east Texas; it is a problem from central Florida across the Gulf states.

WHAT DOES IT LOOK LIKE?

Wood rose is a high-climbing woody vine with hand-shaped leaves divided into seven segments. The showy, trumpet-shaped, morning-glory-like flowers are bright yellow. They are followed by fruits which, when dried, are used in floral arrangements and sold as wood roses.

WHERE DID IT COME FROM? WHERE HAS IT SPREAD?

Wood rose is circumtropical in distribution but is believed to have originated in the tropical Americas. In southern Florida it has become a troublesome pest in hardwood forests, cultivated grounds and overgrown disturbed sites. Infestations of wood rose are sometimes the result of homeowners discarding old floral arrangements that harbor seeds.

WHAT PROBLEMS DOES IT CAUSE?

This twining climber aggressively invades hardwood forests in southern Florida, climbing high into the canopy, often completely enshrouding trees and shrubs and reducing native plant diversity. Fruit productivity is high and seeds remain viable for years. When mature vines are removed and sunlight reaches the forest floor, it is not uncommon to find a new crop of dormant seeds germinating right away.

HOW CAN IT BE CONTROLLED?

Seedlings can be hand-pulled. Mature vines can be controlled by careful basal application of a triclopyr herbicide mixed with an oil diluent. It is especially important to remove seed pods from the site to reduce potential reinfestation. Numerous follow-up inspections and treatments may be required to control this vine.

Roger L. Hammer, Metropolitan Dade County Park and Recreation Department

Wood rose has become a pest in southern Florida's hardwood forests, cultivated grounds and overgrown disturbed sites. Homeowners sometimes discard old floral arrangements harboring seeds, leading to infestations.

VINES

WHAT DOES IT LOOK LIKE?

Water hyacinth is an aquatic herb with cupped leaves and inflated petioles (leaf stems) that enable it to float. White to tan feathery roots extend beneath the plant and may become established in mud along shorelines. Water hyacinth spreads by rhizomes and quickly forms extensive colonies. The showy flowers—violet, with a yellow-centered blue patch in the upper lobe—stand out above the foliage.

WHERE DID IT COME FROM? WHERE HAS IT SPREAD?

Water hyacinth is a native of South America. Shortly after its introduction into the southeastern U.S. in 1884 it escaped cultivation and is now considered one of the most troublesome aquatic weeds in the Gulf states and central California. It inhabits lakes, streams, rivers, bayous, sloughs, canals and other bodies of fresh water.

WHAT PROBLEMS DOES IT CAUSE?

Water hyacinth forms a solid mat on the water surface, crowding out native aquatic vegetation and forming dense shade that kills submerged plants and can alter water temperatures. It reduces habitat value for native wildlife and disrupts the natural food chain by displacing many wildlife species. The plant also impedes recreational boat traffic. Many regard it as the world's worst weed.

HOW CAN IT BE CONTROLLED?

Eichhornia crassipes has proven to be one of the most costly plants to control. When possible, remove plants from small areas by hand or by using a rake. Floating harvester machines are available to remove this species from large bodies of water and canals. If mechanical removal is not feasible, the plants can be sprayed with a glyphosate herbicide approved for aquatic use or 2,4-D, which can only be applied by certified applicators.

Roger L. Hammer, Metropolitan Dade County Park and Recreation Department

Water hyacinth is one of the most troublesome aquatic weeds in the Gulf states and central California, forming a dense mat on waterways.

AQUATIC
PLANTS

FOR MORE INFORMATION

NATIONAL ASSOCIATION OF EXOTIC PEST PLANT COUNCILS (EPPCs)
8208 Dabney Ave.
Springfield, VA 22152
202-682-9400 x230
202-682-1331 (fax)
e-mail: EPPCFTC@aol.com
This is the umbrella organization for the pest plant societies listed below.

CALIFORNIA EXOTIC PEST PLANT COUNCIL
Sally Davis
P.O. Box 15575
Sacramento, CA 95852-0575

FLORIDA EXOTIC PEST PLANT COUNCIL
Amy Ferriter
P.O. Box 24680
West Palm Beach, FL 33416-4680

TENNESSEE EXOTIC PEST PLANT COUNCIL
c/o Friends of Warner Park
50 Vaughn Rd.
Nashville, TN 37221

You can also contact native plant societies for information on invasives in your area. A few are listed below:

CALIFORNIA NATIVE PLANT SOCIETY
Chapter offices throughout the state; for the address of the nearest chapter write:
1722 J St., Suite 17
Sacramento CA 95814
916-447-2677

COLORADO NATIVE PLANT SOCIETY
contact: Andrew Kratz
303-275-5009

VIRGINIA NATIVE PLANT SOCIETY
P.O. Box 844
Annadale, VA 22003

VERMONT EXOTIC SWAT TEAM
c/o Warren King or Liz Thompson
Vermont Field Office
The Nature Conservancy
27 State St.
Montpelier, VT 05672

SOCIETY FOR ECOLOGICAL RESTORATION
University of Wisconsin Arboretum
1207 Seminole Highway
Madison, Wisconsin 53711
608-263-7888
This professional organization of environmental restorationists is open to anyone for membership.

NATURAL AREAS ASSOCIATION
320 South 3rd Street
Rockford, Illinois 61104
815-964-6666
This organization supports the protection and management of natural areas and biodiversity.

For further information on invasives, you can contact the non-profit associations affiliated with many national parks, and Nature Conservancy preserves and field offices throughout the country.

CONTRIBUTORS

MARC ALBERT works with the habitat restoration programs of the Golden Gate National Recreation Area and received his MA in integrative biology from the University of California, Berkeley.

EDWARD R. ALVERSON is Willamette Valley stewardship ecologist for The Nature Conservancy, and is responsible for managing and restoring a number of natural areas in the Valley. He is based in Eugene, Oregon.

SUSAN ANTENEN is director of science and stewardship for The Nature Conservancy on Long Island, New York. She previously directed the Forest Restoration Project at Wave Hill in the Bronx, New York.

STEVEN L. APFELBAUM is a research ecologist with Applied Ecological Services, Inc. and Taylor Creek Restoration Nurseries, in Brodhead, Wisconsin, firms involved in hundreds of ecological restoration projects throughout the U.S. and Canada.

HENRY W. ART is the Samuel Fessenden Clarke Professor of Biology and director of the science division at Williams College in Williamstown, Massachusetts.

GARY BELL is southern California area ecologist for The Nature Conservancy in Temecula, California. He has a PhD in ecology from Carleton University in Ottawa, Canada.

BERND BLOSSEY is director of the Biological Control of Non-indigenous Plant Species Program at New York State College of Agriculture and Life Sciences at Cornell University in Ithaca, New York.

D. DANIEL BOONE is a graduate student in the Appalachian Environment Lab at the University of Maryland. Previously, he worked as a forest ecologist with The Wilderness Society and as the botanist and coordinator of the Maryland Natural Heritage Program.

CARLA BOSSARD is an associate professor of plant ecology at St. Mary's College of California in Moraga and received her PhD in ecology in 1990 from the University of California, Davis. She has written widely about Scotch broom and its establishment in native habitats.

DAVID BOYD is a resource ecologist at the California Department of Parks and Recreation in San Rafael. He has managed several large eucalyptus removal projects.

LAURIE DEITER is integrated pest management coordinator for the City of Boulder Open Space Department where she coordinates the IPM program on 28,000 acres of range, forest and agricultural lands. She was named Weed Manager of the Year in 1993 by the Colorado Weed Management Association.

JOSEPH M. DI TOMASO is assistant non-crop weed specialist in ecology, in the vegetable crops department at the University of California, Davis, where he received his PhD in botany/weed science in 1986.

GLENN D. DREYER is director of the Connecticut College Arboretum and an adjunct associate professor of botany at Connecticut College.

JOHN E. EBINGER is emeritus professor of botany at Eastern Illinois University in Charleston where he has taught for the past 33 years. He received his PhD from Yale University, and for the last three decades has studied the vascular flora and the structure and composition of the forest communities of Illinois.

JAMES A. EIDSON is North Texas land steward for The Nature Conservancy of Texas where he manages five prairie preserves, two suffering from invasion by tall fescue. He has an MS from Texas A&M University where he focused on prairie restoration and control of exotic and invasive species on wildlands.

WILLIAM GLASS is a district heritage biologist with the Illinois Department of Natural Resources, Division of Natural Heritage. He manages state-owned natural areas, including prairie, savannahs, forest and wetlands, and endangered and threatened species habitats in six counties.

ROGER L. HAMMER is a naturalist and resource management supervisor for Metropolitan Dade Parks Department's Natural Areas Management Division and past director of Castellow Hammock Nature Center in South Dade, Florida. He is also chairman of the Native Plant Workshop and author of many articles on the flora of southern Florida.

BETH HANSON edits the handbooks in Brooklyn Botanic Garden's *21st-Century Gardening Series*. She is the former managing editor of the Natural Resources

Defense Council's quarterly publication, *Amicus Journal.*

PATRICIA DALTON HARAGAN is associate curator of the Davies Herbarium at the University of Louisville in Kentucky. For the past 15 years, her research has focused on the weed flora of Kentucky and other parts of the U.S. She is the author of several books including *Weeds of Kentucky and Adjacent States: A Field Guide.*

BONNIE HARPER-LORE is a landscape architect and roadside vegetation coordinator for the Federal Highway Administration where she serves as a technical resource to all 50 state highway agencies. She is a founding member of FICM-NEW (Federal Interagency Committee for the Management of Noxious and Exotic Weeds).

KIM D. HERMAN is stewardship and natural areas coordinator for the natural heritage program of the Michigan Department of Natural Resources in Lansing.

JOHN HUNTER is assistant professor of biological sciences at the State University of New York College at Brockport. He has a PhD in plant biology from the University of California, Davis, and his research focus is the ecology of trees in forests and woodlands.

KRISTINE JOHNSON is resource management specialist at Great Smoky Mountains National Park in Tennessee, and serves on the board of directors of the Tennessee Exotic Pest Plant Council.

ELIZABETH JOHNSON is an ecological consultant. During her eight years with The Nature Conservancy in New Jersey as director of science and stewardship, she managed 17 preserves, each with its own set of invasive weeds. She has an MS from Rutgers University.

GREG JUBINSKY is an environmental program manager with the Florida Department of Environmental Protection. He coordinates statewide use of biological control agents (grass carp and insects) for management of invasive plants and establishes screening methods to prohibit new introductions of invasives.

MIKE KELLY is president of the San Diego conservation group, The Friends of Los Peñasquitos Canyon Preserve. He is also a member of several citizen advisory groups for parks and secretary of the California Exotic Pest Plant Council. He has a BS from San Diego State University.

JILL KENNAY is the natural resources manager at the Natural Land Institute in Rockford, Illinois. She has a degree in ecology from the University of Illinois.

JO KITZ manages the Cold Creek Preserve in the Santa Monica Mountains for Mountains Restoration Trust. She is past-president of the Los Angeles/Santa Monica chapter of the California Native Plant Society.

NORMA KLINE is a conservation biologist, presently working with the Pennsylvania Department of Conservation and Natural Resources.

CAROL LIPPINCOTT, botanist, and SANDRA MCDONALD, weed scientist, are both completing doctoral dissertation research at the University of Florida on the biology, spread, and ecology of cogongrass.

JAMES O. LUKEN is an associate professor in the Department of Biological Sciences at Northern Kentucky University. His research focuses on the physiological and population ecology of invasive woody plants.

JANET MARINELLI is director of publishing at the Brooklyn Botanic Garden. She is the editor of several previous BBG handbooks, including *Going Native: Biodiversity in Our Own Backyards* and *The Environmental Gardener*. She is the author of *The Naturally Elegant Home* and *Your Natural Home*, both published by Little, Brown and Company, and is currently writing a book on the future of gardening in an age of extinction.

BILL MCCLAIN has been involved in natural areas management and research for more than 25 years. His primary interests are prairie and forest communities and exotic species control. As a field biologist, he was responsible for the stewardship of several sites where smooth buckthorn was a management problem.

VICTORIA NUZZO is a natural areas biologist with Native Landscapes in Rockford, Illinois. She specializes in protection, management, and monitoring of natural areas with an emphasis on the spread and control of invasive species.

JOHN M. RANDALL is invasive weed specialist at The Nature Conservancy, where he provides leadership, technical support and advice on weed control to

Nature Conservancy preserves nationwide. He is a founding member, past president and current board member of the California Exotic Pest Plant Council, and a board member of the National Association of Exotic Pest Plant Councils. He holds a PhD in ecology from the University of California, Davis.

SARAH REICHARD is a post-doctoral research fellow in the Department of Zoology at the University of Washington in Seattle. Her research aims to prevent new invasions rather than control existing ones.

PETER RICE is a researcher in the biological sciences division of the University of Montana, in Missoula, where he focuses on introduced species, "a biotic form of pollution."

AMY SAMUELS is a graduate student in the Department of Environmental Forestry and Biology at State University of New York College of Environmental Science and Forestry in Syracuse, New York.

JOHN E. SCHWEGMAN is native plant conservation manager for the Illinois Department of Natural Resources. He received an MA in botany from Southern Illinois University at Carbondale.

LESLIE A. SEIGER has a PhD in ecology from George Washington University, where she wrote her dissertation on the ecology and control of knotweed. She is now studying invasives as a post-doctorate fellow at San Diego State University.

JAKE SIGG is chair of the Invasive Exotics Committee for the California Native Plant Society and is president of its Yerba Buena Chapter. He is retired from Golden Gate Park and Strybing Arboretum and Botanical Gardens, where he supervised the gardening staff and was de facto curator of collections.

GUY STERNBERG, an arborist and landscape architect, is a statewide director of the Illinois Native Plant Society. He runs a research arboretum, Starhill Forest, and has contributed pieces to several of the *Taylor's Guides* garden encyclopedia series, and was co-author and photographer of *Landscaping with Native Trees*.

CAROLYN M. THURMAN is assistant director of science and stewardship for the Pennsylvania Chapter of The Nature Conservancy. Her focus is on site conservation planning and biological monitoring in a management context.

SARA L. WEBB is an associate professor of biology and director of the Environmental Studies Program at Drew University in Madison, New Jersey. Her research interests include the Norway maple invasion, windstorm disturbance to forests and consequences of forest fragmentation for biodiversity.

SANDRA VARDAMAN WELLS is a restoration biologist with the Natural Areas Management Section of the Metropolitan Dade Parks Department where she develops and implements resource management plans for publicly owned natural resource sites in Dade County, Florida.

WILLIAM WIESENBORN is a biologist with the Bureau of Reclamation in Boulder City, Nevada and is interested in biological diversity and water resource planning.

BRIAN WINTER and GORDON YALCH both work in The Nature Conservancy's Minnesota Western Preserves Office; Winter as director of science and stewardship of the Northern Tallgrass Prairie, and Yalch as preserve management assistant.

STEVE YOUNG is a botanist for the New York Natural Heritage Program, where he inventories and studies the state's rare plants. From 1985 to 1990 he was the botanist at the Mercer Arboretum and Botanic Gardens in Houston.

ILLUSTRATION CREDITS

ELLYN MEYERS: cover, 25, 29 left, 38 right, 52, 77, 80, 96

JOHN M. RANDALL: page 1, 9, 19, 45 left and right, 62, 87

JERRY PAVIA: page 5 left, 35, 47, 48, 49, 54, 55, 56, 60, 66, 68, 69, 70, 78, 79, 84, 88, 93, 99

BERND BLOSSEY: page 5 right

ROGER L. HAMMER: page 24, 28, 30, 31, 33, 34, 36, 42, 46, 67, 94, 95, 98

STEVEN CLEMANTS: page 26, 29 right, 64, 65

PAMELA HARPER: page 27, 37, 40, 41 left, 59, 63, 71, 74, 76, 82, 90, 91, 97

DAVID BOYD: page 32

CHRISTINE M. DOUGLAS: page 38 left, 43, 83, 92

BILL GLASS: page 39

BOB HYLAND: page 41 right

CHARLES TURNER: page 44

GREG GAAR: page 50

RHODA LOVE: page 51

JOANNE PAVIA: page 53, 57, 75, 81

PATRICIA DALTON HARAGAN: page 58, 89

JAMES O. LUKEN: page 61

MICHAEL DIRR: page 73

MARC ALBERT: page 72

JOSEPH M. DI TOMASO: page 85, 86

LAURIE DEITER: page 106-107

Russian olive *(Elaeagnus angustifolia)*, a native of Europe and western Asia, has been promoted since the 1930s for windbreaks and erosion control. But it rapidly takes over streambanks, lake shores and wet meadows, and chokes out native cottonwoods and willows, depriving native wildlife of crucial nesting and feeding habitats.

INDEX

⊞ Gardening Books for the Next Century ⊞

Don't miss any of the gardening books in Brooklyn Botanic Garden's 21st-Century Gardening Series! Published four times a year, these award-winning books explore the frontiers of ecological gardening—offering practical, step-by-step tips on creating environmentally sensitive and beautiful gardens for the 1990s and the new century. Your subscription to BBG's 21st-Century Gardening Series is free with Brooklyn Botanic Garden membership.

SUBSCRIPTIONS

To become a member, please call (718) 622-4433, ext. 265. Or photocopy this form, complete and return to: Membership Department, Brooklyn Botanic Garden, 1000 Washington Avenue, Brooklyn, NY 11225-1099.

Your name ....

Address ....

City/State/Zip..Phone ....

AMOUNT

☐ Yes, I want to subscribe to the 21st-Century Gardening Series (4 quarterly volumes) by becoming a member of the Brooklyn Botanic Garden:

☐ $35 (Subscriber)   ☐ $125 (Signature Member)

☐ $50 (Partner)   ☐ $300 (Benefactor) ....

☐ Enclosed is my tax-deductible contribution to the Brooklyn Botanic Garden. ....

TOTAL ....

Form of payment: ☐ Check enclosed ☐ Visa ☐ Mastercard

Credit card# ....Exp ....

Signature...

FOR INFORMATION ON ORDERING ANY OF THE FOLLOWING BACK TITLES, PLEASE WRITE THE
BROOKLYN BOTANIC GARDEN AT THE ABOVE ADDRESS OR CALL (718) 622-4433, EXT. 274.